Donna Kooler's
Cross-Stitch
Christmas

Donna Kooler's
Cross-Stitch Christmas

A Sterling/Chapelle Book
Sterling Publishing Co., Inc. New York

For The Vanessa-Ann Collection

Owner
Jo Packham

Editor
Cherie Hanson

Staff
Trice Boerens, Gaylene Byers,
Holly Fuller, Susan Jorgensen,
Jackie McCowen, Barbara Milburn,
Pamela Randall, Florence Stacey,
Nancy Whitley, and Lorrie Young

Photographers
Ryne Hazen and Gary Rohman

The photographs in this book were taken at The
Loft, Mary Gaskill's Trends and Traditions, and at
the home of Jo Packham, all located in Ogden,
Utah. Their friendly cooperation and trust is deeply
appreciated.

Library of Congress Cataloging-in-Publication Data

Kooler, Donna.
    Donna Kooler's cross-stitch Christmas / Donna Kooler.
        p.   cm.
    "A Sterling/Chapelle book."
    Includes index.
    ISBN 0-8069-0793-2
    1. Cross-stitch—patterns.   2. Christmas decorations.   I. Title.
II. Title: Cross-stitch Christmas.
TT778.C76K66   1994
746.44'3—dc20   94–4191
                                                                  CIP

10 9 8 7 6 5 4 3

A Sterling/Chapelle Book

Published by Sterling Publishing Company, Inc.
387 Park Avenue South, New York, N.Y. 10016
© 1994 by Chapelle Ltd.
Distributed in Canada by Sterling Publishing
c/o Canadian Manda Group, P.O. Box 920, Station U
Toronto, Ontario, Canada M8Z 5P9
Distributed in Great Britain and Europe by Cassell PLC
Villiers House, 41/47 Strand, London WC2N 5JE, England
Distributed in Australia by Capricorn Link (Australia) Pty Ltd.
P.O. Box 6651, Baulkham Hills, Business Centre, NSW 2153, Australia
Printed and bound in Hong Kong
All rights reserved

Sterling ISBN 0-8069-0793-2

Dedication

Dedicated to a wonderful staff, who take joy in
producing holiday memories for you to stitch.

Donna

For Kooler Design Studio, Inc.

President
Donna Kooler

Vice President and Designer
Linda Gillum

Senior Designer
Nancy Rossi

Staff Designers
Barbara Baatz, Holly DeFount, Jorja Hernandez,
and Sandy Orton

Contributing Designer
Donna Yuen

Project Coordinators
Priscilla Timm and Deanna West

Facilitator
Loretta Heden

Design Assistants
Sara Angle, Anita Forfang, Virginia Hanley-Rivett,
Vivian Harlin, Marsha Hinkson, Arlis Johnson,
Lori Patton, Char Randolph, Giana Tarricone,
and Pam Whyte

Contributing Project Constructionist
Laurie Grant

*For information on where to purchase specialty
items in this book, please write to Customer Service
Department, Chapelle Designers, 204 25th Street,
Suite 300, Ogden, UT 84401.*

🌲🌲🌲🌲🌲🌲🌲🌲🌲🌲🌲🌲🌲🌲🌲🌲🌲🌲🌲🌲

Merry Christmas

What could be more delightful and rewarding to stitchers than a home filled with their own lovingly stitched ornaments, stockings, pictures, and pillows, or receiving a handmade gift from a fellow stitch enthusiast? All of the designs and projects, created by the Kooler Design Staff and presented in this book, celebrate the joy and wonder of this special time.

From an exquisite, full-sized Elegant Nutcracker Stocking or classic Winter Wonderland Santa picture to a small doll's pinafore decorated with holly or a whimsical Mouse Tree House Ornament, each design is as merry and bright as the holiday season itself and is sure to delight both the young and the young at heart.

From all of us at Kooler Design Studio, we wish you the merriest of Christmases and many completed cross-stitched projects in the new year.

CONTENTS

The whole world is a Christmas tree,
and stars it's many candles be.

GOOD LI'L GIRLS & BOYS STOCKINGS

Stitched on white Aida 14 for Santa & animals, ivory Aida 14 for Santa & toys over one thread, the finished design size is 10¼" x 15¾" for Santa & animals, 10⅛" x 15⅝" for Santa & toys. The fabric was cut 15" x 20" for both.

SANTA & ANIMALS

FABRICS	DESIGN SIZES
Aida 11	13" x 20⅛"
Aida 18	8" x 12¼"
Hardanger 22	6½" x 10"

SANTA & TOYS

FABRICS	DESIGN SIZES
Aida 11	12⅞" x 19⅞"
Aida 18	7⅞" x 12⅛"
Hardanger 22	6½" x 9⅞"

MATERIALS *(for one stocking)*

Completed design on ivory Aida 14 (Santa & toys), white Aida 14 (Santa & animals)
½ yard of red fabric; matching thread
½ yard of red print fabric for lining
Cotton embroidery floss
#22 tapestry needle
1¼ yards of ⅛"-diameter cotton cord
Dressmaker's pen

DIRECTIONS

All seams are ½".

1. Enlarge the pattern on the grid on page 11 to make a full-size pattern. Cut out. Place the pattern on the design piece with the top edge of the pattern 1⅞" above and parallel to the top row of stitching. Cut out the stocking front. From red fabric, cut one stocking for back, cut one 2" x 5" piece for hanger, and cut 1½"-wide bias strips, piecing as needed to equal 60". From red print, cut two stockings for lining front and back.

2. Make piping, using cotton cord and 1½"-wide bias strips.

3. With raw edges aligned, stitch the piping down the side, around the bottom, and up the other side of the stocking front. With right sides together, stitch the stocking front to the back, sewing along the stitching line of the piping. Leave the top edge open. Trim seams; turn.

4. With right sides facing and edges aligned, stitch the lining front and back together, leaving the top edge open and an opening in the side seam above the heel. Do not turn.

5. To make hanger, fold 2" x 5" piece in half lengthwise, with right sides facing and long edges aligned. Stitch long edges. Turn. With seam at back center, fold hanger in half, forming a loop. Press. With raw edges matching, pin the loop to the top right side seam of the stocking.

6. Slide the lining over the stocking, right sides together. Stitch around the top edge of the stocking, securing the hanger. Turn the stocking right side out through the side opening in the lining. Slipstitch the opening closed. Slide the lining inside the stocking.

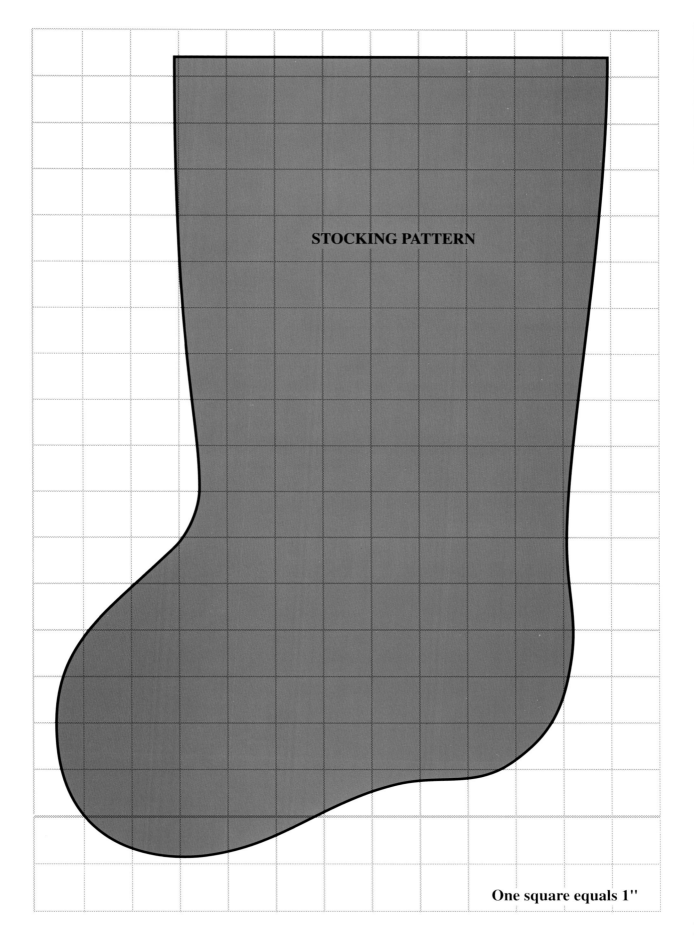

STOCKING PATTERN

One square equals 1"

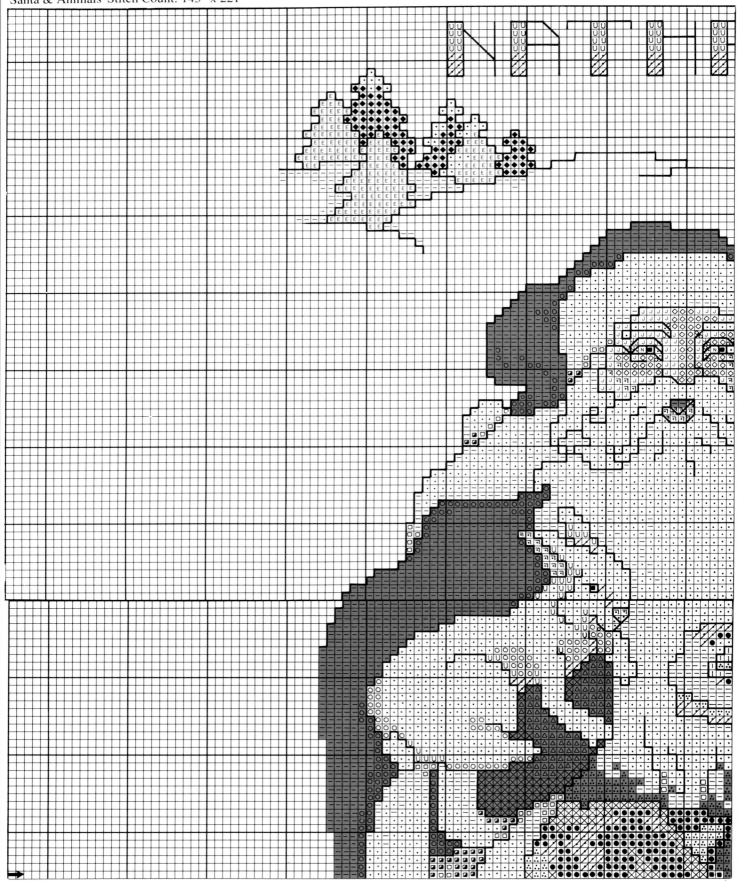

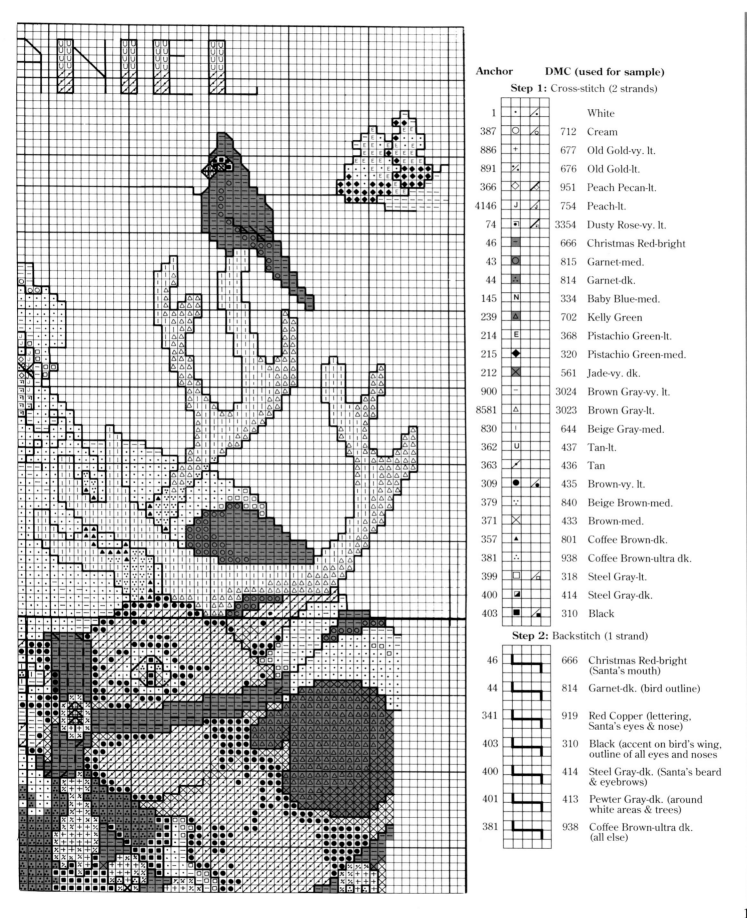

Anchor			DMC (used for sample)
			Step 1: Cross-stitch (2 strands)
1	·	⁄·	White
387	○	⁄○	712 Cream
886	+		677 Old Gold-vy. lt.
891	⅌		676 Old Gold-lt.
366	◇	⁄◇	951 Peach Pecan-lt.
4146	J	⁄J	754 Peach-lt.
74	⊡	⁄⊡	3354 Dusty Rose-vy. lt.
46	⊟		666 Christmas Red-bright
43	◎		815 Garnet-med.
44	⁚⁚		814 Garnet-dk.
145	N		334 Baby Blue-med.
239	△		702 Kelly Green
214	E		368 Pistachio Green-lt.
215	◆		320 Pistachio Green-med.
212	⊠		561 Jade-vy. dk.
900	–		3024 Brown Gray-vy. lt.
8581	△		3023 Brown Gray-lt.
830	I		644 Beige Gray-med.
362	U		437 Tan-lt.
363	⁄		436 Tan
309	●	⁄●	435 Brown-vy. lt.
379	⁚⁚		840 Beige Brown-med.
371	⊗		433 Brown-med.
357	▲		801 Coffee Brown-dk.
381	∴		938 Coffee Brown-ultra dk.
399	□	⁄◹	318 Steel Gray-lt.
400	◩		414 Steel Gray-dk.
403	■	⁄■	310 Black

Step 2: Backstitch (1 strand)

46	666	Christmas Red-bright (Santa's mouth)
44	814	Garnet-dk. (bird outline)
341	919	Red Copper (lettering, Santa's eyes & nose)
403	310	Black (accent on bird's wing, outline of all eyes and noses
400	414	Steel Gray-dk. (Santa's beard & eyebrows)
401	413	Pewter Gray-dk. (around white areas & trees)
381	938	Coffee Brown-ultra dk. (all else)

13

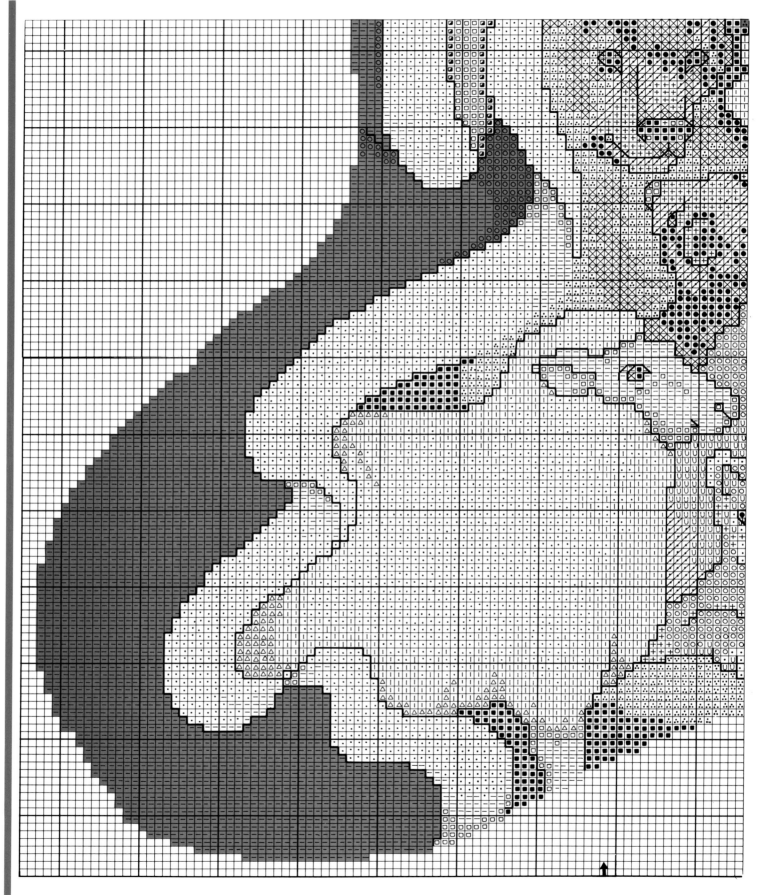

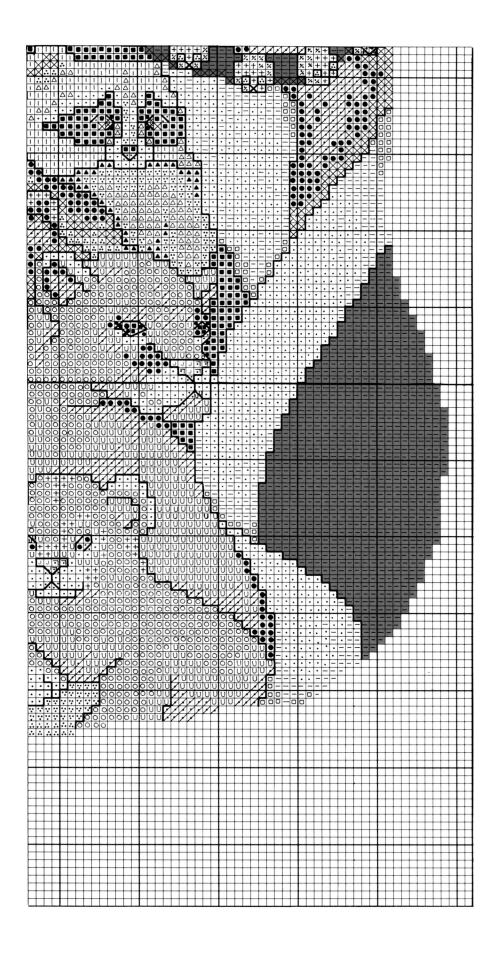

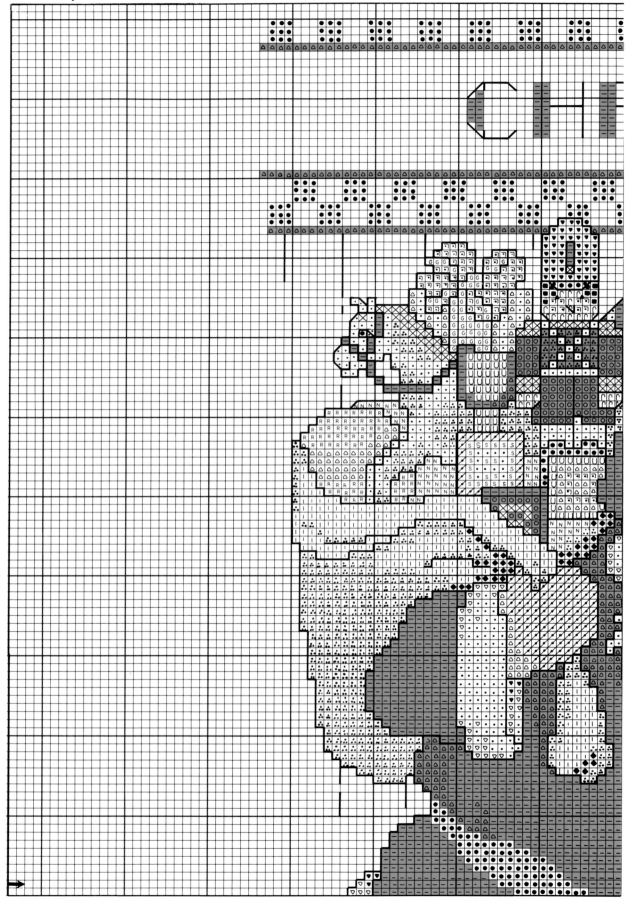

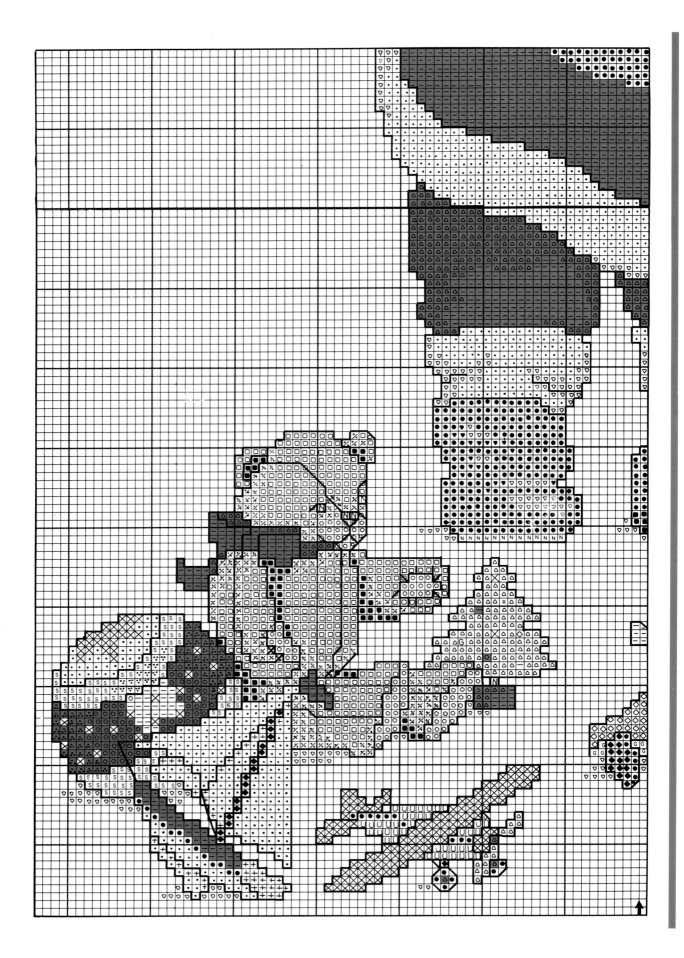

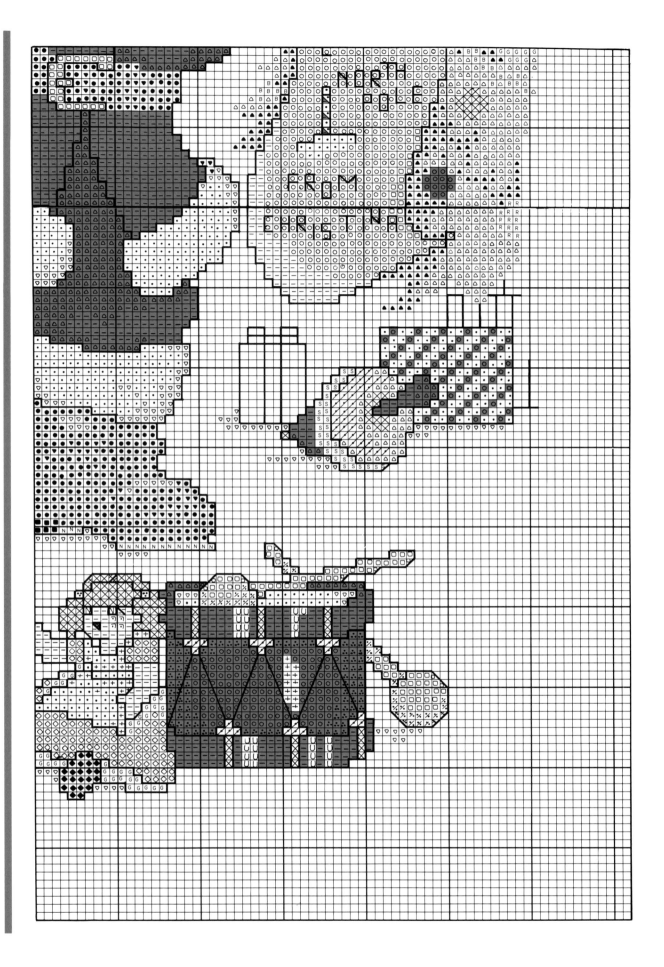

Anchor   **DMC (used for sample)**

Step 1: Cross-stitch (2 strands)

Anchor			DMC	Color
1	·	⁄		White
387	O	⁄	712	Cream
292	B	⁄	3078	Golden Yellow-vy. lt.
297	✕		743	Yellow-med.
880	–		948	Peach-vy. lt.
8	⌐	⁄	353	Peach
316	U	⁄	970	Pumpkin-lt.
24	◹		776	Pink-med.
75	∵		604	Cranberry-lt.
76	S		603	Cranberry
74	◇	⁄	3354	Dusty Rose-vy. lt.
49	G		962	Wild Rose-med.
46	▬		666	Christmas Red-bright
43	△		815	Garnet-med.
98	R		553	Violet-med.
158	+		775	Baby Blue-vy. lt.
145	◉		334	Baby Blue-med.
164	⁙		824	Blue-vy. dk.
256	⁄		704	Chartreuse-bright
239	◮		702	Kelly Green
212	▲		561	Jade-vy. dk.
388	l		3033	Mocha Brown-vy. lt.
392	∴		642	Beige Gray-dk.
362	☐	⁄	437	Tan-lt.
363	⁒	⁄	436	Tan
370	■	⁄	434	Brown-lt.
379	◆		840	Beige Brown-med.
357	N		801	Coffee Brown-dk.
397	T	⁄	762	Pearl Gray-vy. lt.
399	▽		318	Steel Gray-lt.
400	▼	⁄	414	Steel Gray-dk.
403	●	⁄	310	Black

Step 2: Long Loose Stitch

Anchor		DMC	Color
401		413	Pewter Gray-dk.—one strand (earpiece of glasses)
297		743	Yellow-med.—three strands (on drum)
403		310	Black—one strand (rigging of boat) —three strands (bow of boat)

Step 3: Backstitch (1 strand)

Anchor		DMC	Color
46		666	Christmas Red-bright (Santa's mouth, list)
43		815	Garnet-med. (red, rose areas of Santa, doll, bear, tree base, drum, top, horse's reins, bow)
212		561	Jade-vy. dk. (green areas of toys, gloves; box, ball in Santa's bag)
164		824	Blue-vy. dk. (outline of blue areas of drum, ball, box, soldier, doll's apron)
370		434	Brown-lt. (lines inside bear, outline of doll's hair)
401		413	Pewter Gray-dk. (outline of white and gray areas of Santa; horse, candycane, pole, ball, outline of boat box, blocks, soldier's hat)
403		310	Black (outline of airplane, wheels, top of doll's shoe, Santa's boots, belt)
46		666	Christmas Red-bright—two strands (name on stocking)
357		801	Coffee Brown-dk. (outline, face lines of bear, outline of airplane, doll's arms, face, eyes, shoes, drumsticks, box lines, cream area of Santa's list, star, fireplace, wall lines, brown areas of Santa's bag, Santa's eyes, nose, ear, soles of shoes, soldier's head, nose, arms, legs)

Step 4: French Knot (1 strand)

Anchor		DMC	Color
46	●	666	Christmas Red-bright (Santa's list)
403	▲	310	Black (soldier's eyes)

This alphabet is graphed in two colors and is used on the Santa and animals stocking. The alphabet for the Santa and toys stocking uses this graph and only one color.

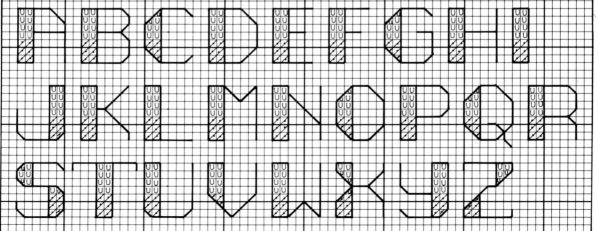

At Christmas play & make good cheer,
for Christmas comes but once a year.

GOOD LI'L GIRLS & BOYS ORNAMENTS

Stitched on cream Aida 18 over one thread, the finished design size is 2" x 2½" for the teddy bear, and 2" x 2½" for the doll. The fabric was cut 4" x 5" for the teddy bear, and 6" x 6" for the doll.

TEDDY BEAR

FABRICS	DESIGN SIZES
Aida 11	3⅜" x 4"
Aida 14	2⅝" x 3⅛"
Hardanger 22	1⅝" x 2"

DOLL

FABRICS	DESIGN SIZES
Aida 11	5¼" x 3"
Aida 14	4⅛" x 2¼"
Hardanger 22	2⅝" x 1½"

MATERIALS *(for one ornament)*
Completed design on cream Aida 18
¼ yard of black gingham fabric
¼ yard of red fabric
5" square of heavyweight cardboard
5" square of lightweight cardboard
5" square of fleece
6" of ⅛"-wide red satin ribbon
6" of ¹⁄₁₆"-wide red satin ribbon
15" of ³⁄₁₆"-diameter cotton cord
Sewing thread: red and white
Two ¼"-diameter brass jingle bells
Red perle cotton or floss
Glue
Tracing paper

DIRECTIONS
1. Trace and cut out ornament pattern on page 23. From heavyweight cardboard, cut one ornament. From lightweight cardboard, cut one ornament. From fleece, cut one ornament. From black gingham fabric, cut one ornament, adding 1" to all edges. Also from black gingham fabric, cut 2"-wide bias strips, piecing as needed to equal 25". With design piece centered, cut one ornament, adding 1" to all edges. From red fabric, cut 1½"-wide bias strips, piecing as needed to equal 15".

2. Lightly glue fleece to heavyweight cardboard.

3. Center fleece/cardboard over wrong side of design. Pulling snugly, wrap and glue edges to cardboard back.

4. Center lightweight cardboard over wrong side of black gingham fabric. Pulling snugly, wrap and glue edges to cardboard back.

5. Make piping, using cotton cord and red bias strips.

6. Glue piping around back edge of design/cardboard, overlapping ends at center bottom.

7. With right sides facing, sew short sides of black gingham bias strips together, making a loop. Press seam open.

8. Fold strip in half lengthwise and press. Sew two rows of gathering stitches, ⅛" from raw edges. Gather to fit perimeter of design/cardboard piece. Glue gathered edge of ruffle to edge of cardboard back of design piece.

9. Fold ⅛" red ribbon in half to form a loop for hanger and glue raw ends to back of design/cardboard at center top edge.

10. Glue wrong sides of design/cardboard and fabric/cardboard together. Weight with brick or book until glue is dry.

11. Tie each bell to one 2" length of perle cotton; place small dab of glue over knot to secure. Tie bells together at varying lengths. Glue bell grouping to center bottom of piping.

12. Tie ¹⁄₁₆"-wide red ribbon into small bow and glue over knot of bell grouping. Trim ends.

ORNAMENT PATTERN

Anchor		DMC (used for sample)	
Step 1: Cross-stitch (2 strands)			
1	· ⁄		White
387	○ ⁄	712	Cream
46	−	666	Christmas Red-bright
43	△	815	Garnet-med.
362	□ ⁄	437	Tan-lt.
363	⁒ ⁄	436	Tan
370	■ ◢	434	Brown-lt.
357	N	801	Coffee Brown-dk.
399	▽	318	Steel Gray-lt.

Anchor		DMC	
Step 2: Backstitch (1 strand)			
43		815	Garnet-med. (bow, hat)
370		434	Brown-lt. (lines inside bear)
357		801	Coffee Brown-dk. (outline, bear's face)
401		413	Pewter Gray-dk. (outline on white of hat)

Teddy Bear
Stitch Count: 37" x 44"

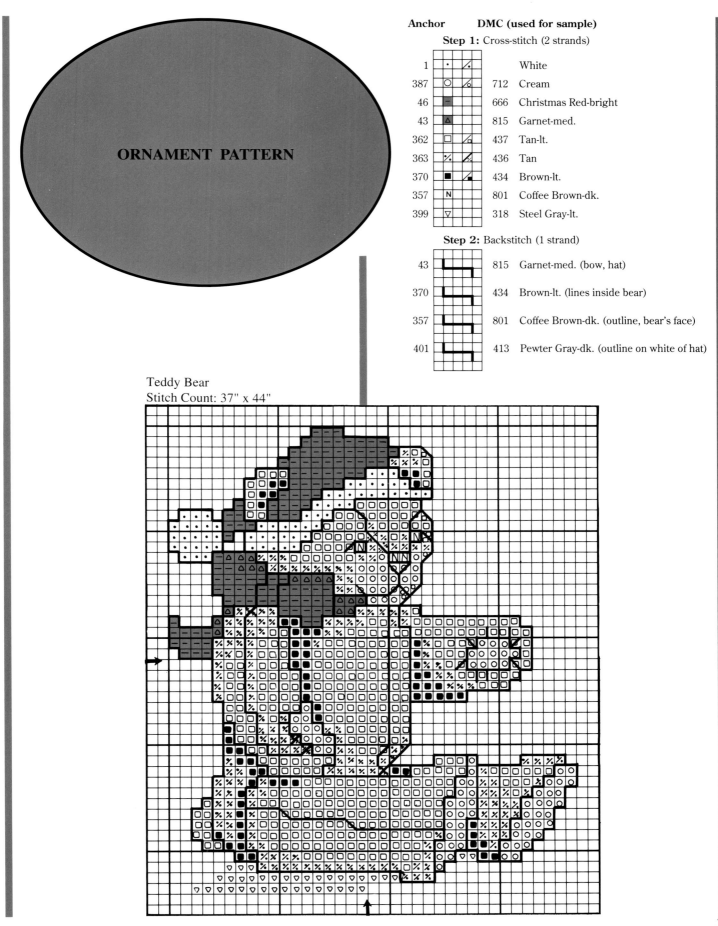

23

ANTIQUE CHRISTMAS TOYS

Stitched on cream Quaker cloth 28 over two threads, the finished design size is 11" x 7½". The fabric was cut 17" x 14".

FABRICS
Aida 11
Aida 14
Aida 18
Hardanger 22

DESIGN SIZES
14" x 9½"
11" x 7½"
8½" x 5⅞"
7" x 4¾"

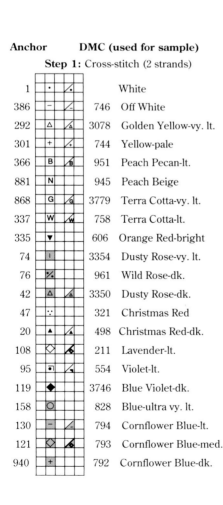

Anchor			DMC (used for sample)	
Step 1: Cross-stitch (2 strands)				
1	·	⁄		White
386	−	⁄	746	Off White
292	△	◿	3078	Golden Yellow-vy. lt.
301	+	⁄	744	Yellow-pale
366	B	◿	951	Peach Pecan-lt.
881	N		945	Peach Beige
868	G	◿	3779	Terra Cotta-vy. lt.
337	W	◿	758	Terra Cotta-lt.
335	▼		606	Orange Red-bright
74	I		3354	Dusty Rose-vy. lt.
76	⁒		961	Wild Rose-dk.
42	△	◿	3350	Dusty Rose-dk.
47	∴		321	Christmas Red
20	▲	◿	498	Christmas Red-dk.
108	◇	◿	211	Lavender-lt.
95	▫	⁄	554	Violet-lt.
119	◆		3746	Blue Violet-dk.
158	○		828	Blue-ultra vy. lt.
130	−	⁄	794	Cornflower Blue-lt.
121	◇	◿	793	Cornflower Blue-med.
940	+		792	Cornflower Blue-dk.

Anchor			DMC	
941	∵		791	Cornflower Blue-vy. dk.
265	·	◿	3348	Yellow Green-lt.
243	□	◿	988	Forest Green-med.
246	✕	◿	986	Forest Green-vy. dk.
942	I		738	Tan-vy. lt.
362	U	◿	437	Tan-lt.
363	○	◿	436	Tan
347	⁄		402	Mahogany-vy. lt.
324	□	◿	922	Copper-lt.
349	✕		301	Mahogany-med.
370	S	◿	434	Brown-lt.
936	■	◿	632	Pecan-dk.
393	⁒		3790	Beige Gray-ultra vy. dk.
397	▽	◿	762	Pearl Gray-vy. lt.
399	T	◿	318	Steel Gray-lt.
400	∴	◿	317	Pewter Gray
403	●	◿	310	Black

Step 2: Backstitch (1 strand)

Anchor		DMC	
42	⌐	3350	Dusty Rose-dk. (doll's hat, pink in doll's dress, doll's mouth)
941	⌐	791	Cornflower Blue-vy. dk. (bow in doll's hat, bear's hat, blue in bear's clothes)
246	⌐	986	Forest Green-vy. dk. (saddle, green on mouse, rockers)
349	⌐	301	Mahogany-med. (doll's hair, doll's hands, lines on floor, balls, doll's face)
936	⌐	632	Pecan-dk. (horse, bear)
400	⌐	317	Pewter Gray (doll's eyes, gray in doll's dress, bow and cuffs in bear's shirt, mouse)
403	⌐	310	Black (doll's shoes)

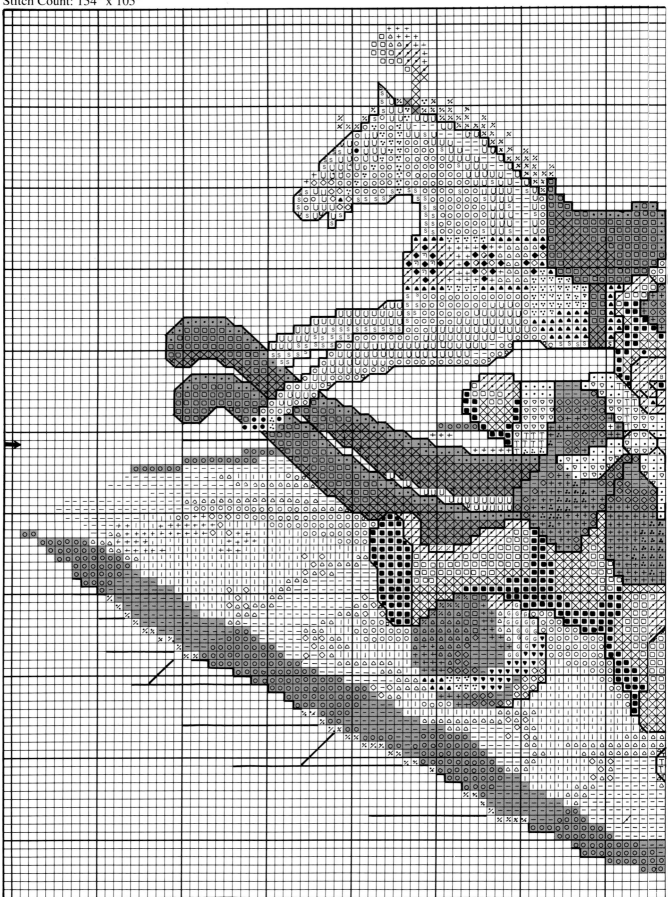

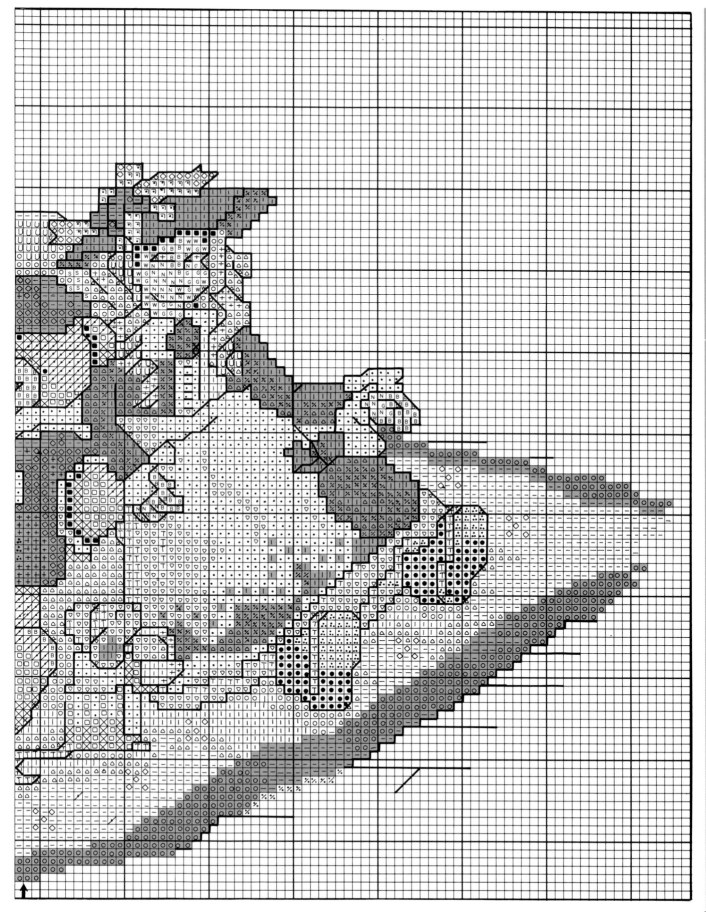

May your Christmas be a
celebration of friendship & love.

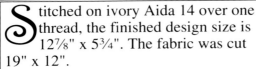RIENDSHIP PILLOW

Stitched on ivory Aida 14 over one thread, the finished design size is 12⅞" x 5¾". The fabric was cut 19" x 12".

FABRICS	DESIGN SIZES
Aida 11	16⅜" x 7⅜"
Aida 18	10" x 4½"
Hardanger 22	8⅛" x 3⅝"

MATERIALS
Completed design on ivory Aida 14
½ yard of blue gingham fabric
2½ yards of 5"-wide cream flat eyelet trim
1½ yards of ³⁄₁₆"-diameter cotton cord
9" x 16" piece of fleece
Perle cotton or buttonhole thread
Ivory sewing thread
Polyester stuffing

DIRECTIONS
All seams are ½".

1. Trim design fabric 1⅛" beyond white square corner motifs on all sides. Using design fabric as pattern, cut one pillow back from blue gingham fabric and one pillow back from fleece. From remaining blue gingham fabric, cut 1½" bias strips, piecing as needed to equal 50".

2. Make piping using cotton cord and bias strips.

3. Baste fleece to back of design piece. Trim edges.

4. Aligning raw edges, baste piping around right side of design piece, overlapping ends at center bottom.

5. With right sides facing, sew ends of eyelet trim to form loop. To gather, zigzag-stitch over length of perle cotton thread ⅜" from raw edge of trim. Pull thread, gathering ruffle to fit perimeter of design piece.

6. With right sides facing and raw edges matching, baste ruffle to design piece, allowing more gathers at corners.

7. With right sides together, sew design piece and pillow back together, leaving a 6" opening at bottom. Clip corners and turn right side out. Stuff firmly. Slipstitch opening closed.

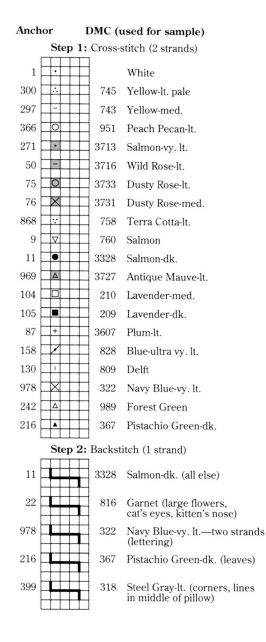

Anchor | **DMC (used for sample)**

Step 1: Cross-stitch (2 strands)

Anchor		DMC	
1	·		White
300	∴	745	Yellow-lt. pale
297	−	743	Yellow-med.
366	◯	951	Peach Pecan-lt.
271	▪	3713	Salmon-vy. lt.
50	⊟	3716	Wild Rose-lt.
75	◯	3733	Dusty Rose-lt.
76	✕	3731	Dusty Rose-med.
868	∴	758	Terra Cotta-lt.
9	▽	760	Salmon
11	●	3328	Salmon-dk.
969	△	3727	Antique Mauve-lt.
104	▫	210	Lavender-med.
105	▪	209	Lavender-dk.
87	+	3607	Plum-lt.
158	╱	828	Blue-ultra vy. lt.
130	ı	809	Delft
978	✕	322	Navy Blue-vy. lt.
242	△	989	Forest Green
216	▲	367	Pistachio Green-dk.

Step 2: Backstitch (1 strand)

11		3328	Salmon-dk. (all else)
22		816	Garnet (large flowers, cat's eyes, kitten's nose)
978		322	Navy Blue-vy. lt.—two strands (lettering)
216		367	Pistachio Green-dk. (leaves)
399		318	Steel Gray-lt. (corners, lines in middle of pillow)

Stitch Count: 180" x 81"

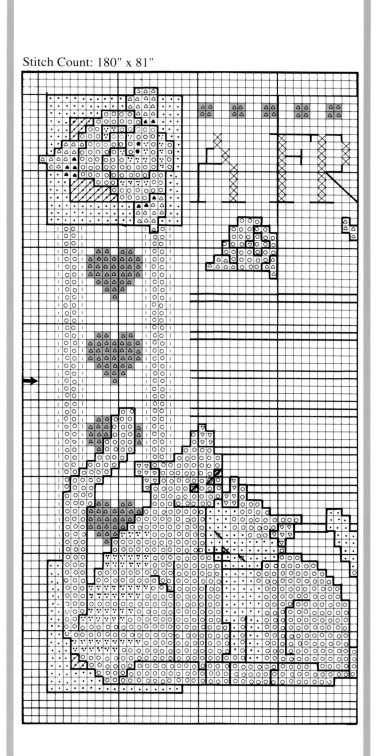

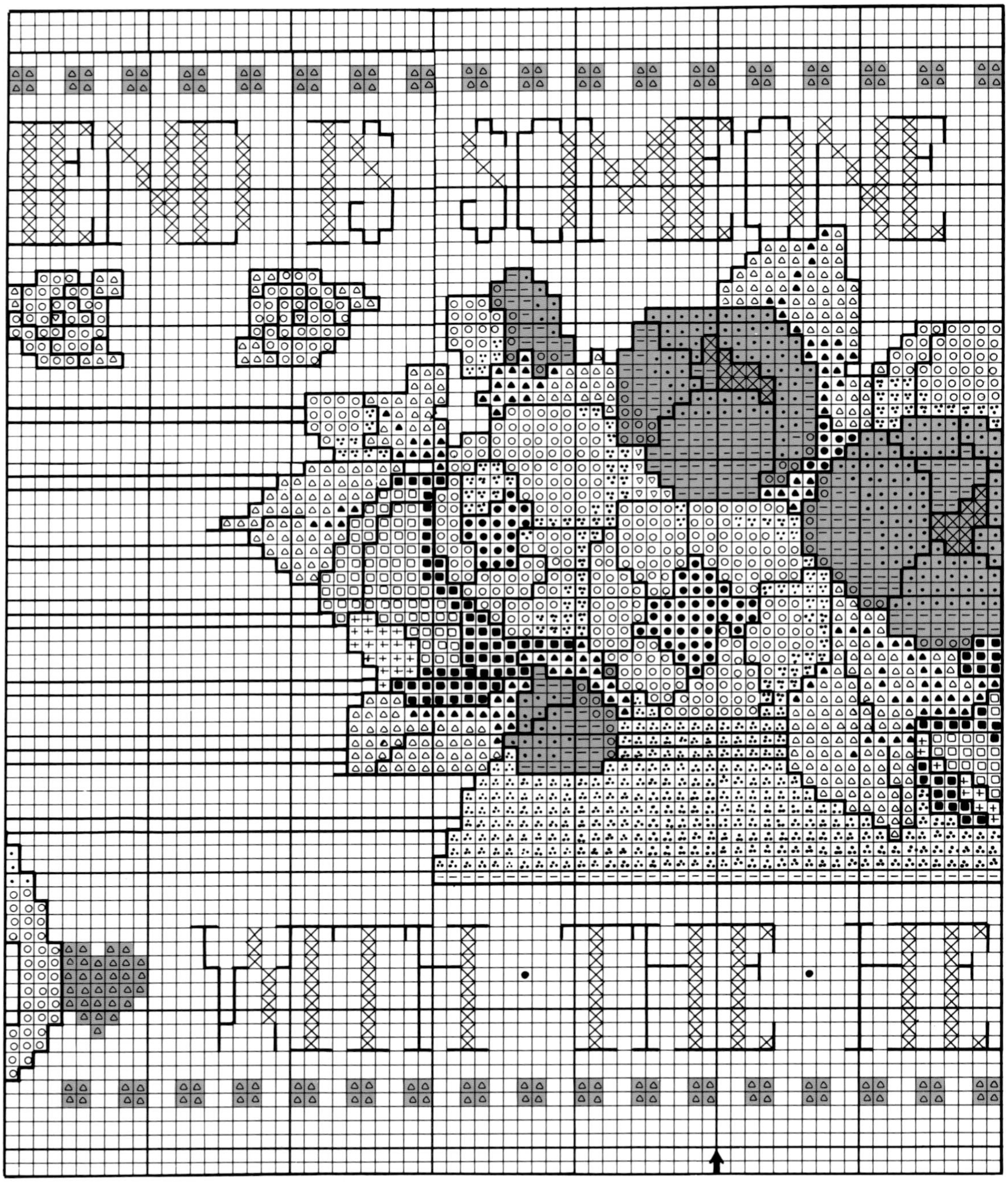
END IS SOMEONE
WITH · THE · HE

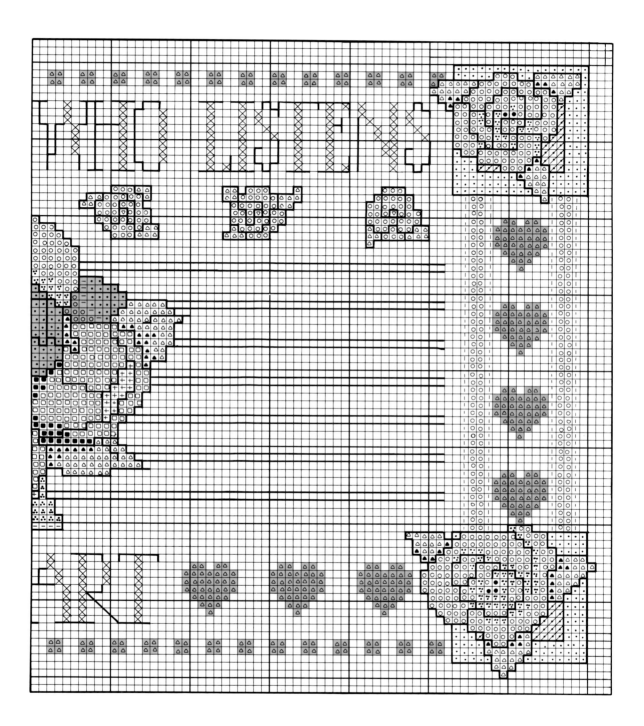

Friendship Trio Ornaments

Stitched on ivory Aida 18 over one thread, the finished design size is 2³⁄₈" x 2½" for #1, 2¼" x 2³⁄₈" for #2, 1⁷⁄₈" x 2¾" for #3. The fabric was cut 9" x 9".

#1
FABRICS	DESIGN SIZES
Aida 11	3⁷⁄₈" x 4"
Aida 14	3" x 3¹⁄₈"
Hardanger 22	1⁷⁄₈" x 2"

#2
FABRICS	DESIGN SIZES
Aida 11	3⁵⁄₈" x 4"
Aida 14	2⁷⁄₈" x 3¹⁄₈"
Hardanger 22	1⁷⁄₈" x 2"

#3
FABRICS	DESIGN SIZES
Aida 11	3" x 4½"
Aida 14	2³⁄₈" x 3½"
Hardanger 22	1½" x 2¼"

Anchor		DMC (used for sample)	

Step 1: Backstitch (1 strand)

Anchor	DMC	Color
76	3731	Dusty Rose-med. (flowers)
22	816	Garnet ("Christmas" on #1, lettering on #3)
978	322	Navy Blue-vy. lt. (lettering on #2)
242	989	Forest Green (lettering on #1, leaves on #3)
216	367	Pistachio Green-dk. (leaves on #1 & #2)
399	318	Steel Gray-lt. (cats)

Step 2: French Knot (1 strand)

Anchor	DMC	Color
22	816	Garnet
242	989	Forest Green

MATERIALS (for one ornament)
Completed design on ivory Aida 18
¼ yard of blue gingham fabric
4" square of heavyweight cardboard
4" square of lightweight cardboard
4" square of fleece
6" of ⅛"-wide cream satin ribbon
4" of ⅜"-wide peach satin ribbon
3" of ¼"-wide green satin ribbon
12" of ¾"-wide pre-gathered cream eyelet trim
12" of ³⁄₁₆"-diameter cotton cord
Ivory sewing thread
Small mauve ribbon rose
Glue
Tracing paper

DIRECTIONS
1. Trace and cut out ornament pattern on page 35 appropriate for design. From heavyweight cardboard, cut one ornament. From lightweight cardboard, cut one ornament. From fleece, cut one ornament. From blue gingham fabric, cut one ornament, adding ½" to all edges. Also from blue gingham fabric, cut 1½"-wide bias strips, piecing as needed to equal 14".

2. Lightly glue fleece to heavyweight cardboard.

3. Center fleece/cardboard over wrong side of design. Pulling snugly, wrap and glue edges to cardboard back.

4. Center lightweight cardboard over wrong side of blue gingham fabric. Pulling snugly, wrap and glue edges to cardboard back.

5. Make piping, using cotton cord and 1½"-wide bias strips.

6. Glue piping around back edge of design/cardboard, overlapping ends at center bottom.

7. Glue eyelet trim around back edge of design/cardboard, overlapping ends at center bottom and folding top raw end under ½".

8. Fold cream ribbon in half to form a loop for hanger and glue raw ends to back of design/cardboard at center top edge.

9. Glue wrong sides of design/cardboard and fabric/cardboard together. Weight with brick or book until glue is dry.

10. With right sides together, stitch peach ribbon ends to form a loop. Hand-sew running stitch along one side, gather, and secure thread. Loop green ribbon, pinching and gluing at center to form leaves. Tack leaves to center of gathered peach ribbon. Tack ribbon rose to center of gathered peach ribbon. Tack rose to eyelet at center top of ornament.

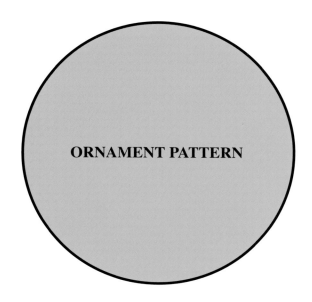

ORNAMENT PATTERN

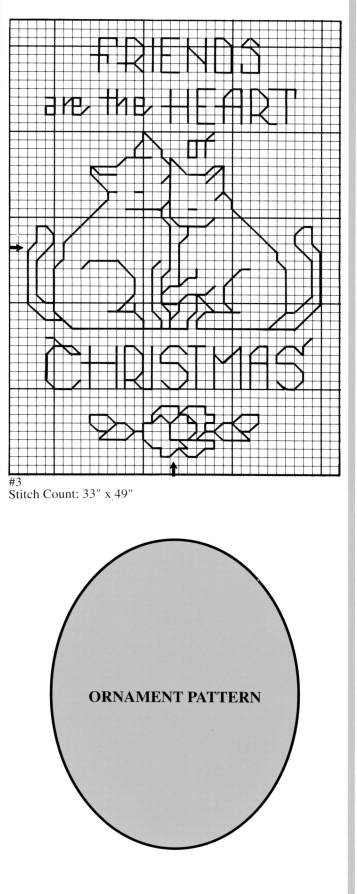

#3
Stitch Count: 33" x 49"

ORNAMENT PATTERN

#1
Stitch Count: 42" x 44"

#2
Stitch Count: 40" x 43"

Once on a December night,
an angel held a candle bright.

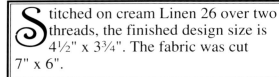OVEBIRDS PLACEMAT

Stitched on cream Linen 26 over two threads, the finished design size is 4½" x 3¾". The fabric was cut 7" x 6".

FABRICS DESIGN SIZES

FABRICS	DESIGN SIZES
Aida 11	5⅛" x 4⅜"
Aida 14	4⅛" x 3⅜"
Aida 18	3⅛" x 2⅝"
Hardanger 22	2⅝" x 2⅛"

MATERIALS

Completed design on cream Linen 26
¾ yard of brown polished cotton; matching thread
¼ yard of cream fabric; matching thread
⅜ yard of fleece

DIRECTIONS

All seams are ½".

1. From brown polished cotton, cut two 12½" x 20" pieces for placemat front and back. Also from brown polished cotton, cut ½"-wide bias strips, piecing as needed to equal 71". From fleece, cut one 12½" x 20" piece. From cream fabric, cut one 6" x 6¾" piece for design facing. With design piece centered, trim to 6" x 6¾".

2. With right sides facing and edges aligned, sew design and facing pieces together along seam on right edge of design only. Turn and press seam inward. With right sides facing and edges aligned, sew bias strip border to design piece along top edge only. Double-fold bias strip ¼" to back and slipstitch, covering stitching line.

3. Place design/facing piece on lower left edge of front placemat piece, easing bottom edge of design/facing piece and aligning left edge. Topstitch right edge in place on placemat. Baste left and bottom edge in place.

4. Baste fleece to wrong side of placemat front.

5. With wrong sides facing and edges aligned, baste placemat front and back pieces together.

6. With right sides facing and edges aligned, stitch bias-strip border to placemat front along all edges and mitering each corner. Double-fold bias strip ¼" to back and slipstitch, covering stitching line and mitering corners.

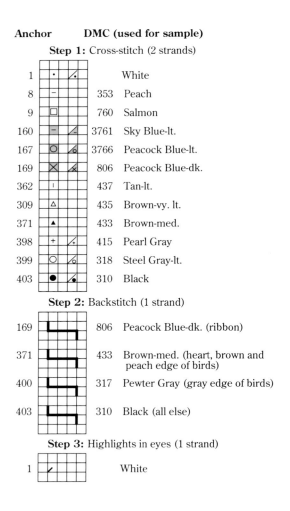

Anchor	DMC (used for sample)	
	Step 1: Cross-stitch (2 strands)	
1		White
8	353	Peach
9	760	Salmon
160	3761	Sky Blue-lt.
167	3766	Peacock Blue-lt.
169	806	Peacock Blue-dk.
362	437	Tan-lt.
309	435	Brown-vy. lt.
371	433	Brown-med.
398	415	Pearl Gray
399	318	Steel Gray-lt.
403	310	Black
	Step 2: Backstitch (1 strand)	
169	806	Peacock Blue-dk. (ribbon)
371	433	Brown-med. (heart, brown and peach edge of birds)
400	317	Pewter Gray (gray edge of birds)
403	310	Black (all else)
	Step 3: Highlights in eyes (1 strand)	
1		White

Stitch Count: 57" x 48"

ANGELIC ORNAMENTS

Stitched on navy Aida 14 over one thread, the finished design size is 3¾" x 3¾". The fabric was cut 6" x 6".

FABRICS	DESIGN SIZES
Aida 11	4¾" x 4¾"
Aida 14	3¾" x 3¾"
Aida 18	3" x 3"
Hardanger 22	2⅜" x 2⅜"

MATERIALS *(for one ornament)*
Completed design on navy Aida 14
⅓ yard of gold foil lamé
4" square of heavyweight cardboard
4" square of lightweight cardboard
4" square of fleece
6" of ⅛"-wide metallic gold grosgrain ribbon
18" of ³⁄₁₆"-diameter cotton cord
Yellow sewing thread
One 3½"-long metallic gold tassel
One small gold ribbon rose
Glue
Tracing paper

DIRECTIONS
1. Trace and cut out ornament pattern. From heavyweight cardboard, cut one ornament. From lightweight cardboard, cut one ornament. From fleece, cut one ornament. From gold lamé, cut one ornament, adding 1" to all edges. Also from gold lamé, cut 1½"-wide bias strips, piecing as needed to equal 18". With design piece centered, cut one ornament, adding 1" to all edges.

2. Lightly glue fleece to heavyweight cardboard.

3. Center fleece/cardboard over wrong side of design. Pulling snugly, wrap and glue edges to cardboard back.

4. Center lightweight cardboard over wrong side of gold lamé. Pulling snugly, wrap and glue edges to cardboard back.

5. Make piping, using cotton cord and gold lamé bias strips.

6. Glue piping around back edge of design/cardboard, overlapping ends at center bottom.

7. Fold ⅛" gold ribbon in half to form a loop for hanger and glue raw ends to back of design/cardboard at center top edge.

8. Glue tassel to back of design/cardboard at center bottom edge.

9. Glue wrong sides of design/cardboard and fabric/cardboard together. Weight with brick or book until glue is dry.

10. Tack ribbon rose to center top of piping.

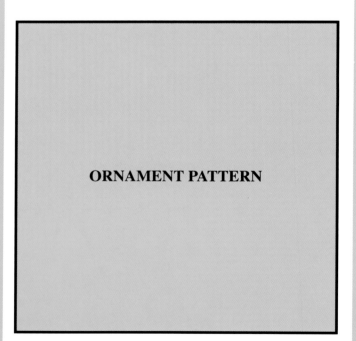

ORNAMENT PATTERN

Anchor			DMC (used for sample)	
			Step 1: Cross-stitch (2 strands)	
1	· /			White
300	+ /		745	Yellow-lt. pale
301	□		744	Yellow-pale
307	∴		783	Christmas Gold
881	O /		945	Peach Beige
868	— /		758	Terra Cotta-lt.
5975	✕ ✕		356	Terra Cotta-med.
333	/		608	Orange Red
47	▲		321	Christmas Red
43	∴		815	Garnet-med.

128	—		800	Delft-pale
130	△		799	Delft-med.
131	O		798	Delft-dk.
921	⊠		931	Antique Blue-med.
355	● /		975	Golden Brown-dk.
900	∣ /		928	Slate Green-lt.
	▽		002HL	Kreinik Fine #8 Braid Gold

Step 2: Backstitch (1 strand)

132		797	Royal Blue (wings, ribbon)
905		3031	Mocha Brown-vy. dk. (all else)

Stitch Count: 53" x 53"

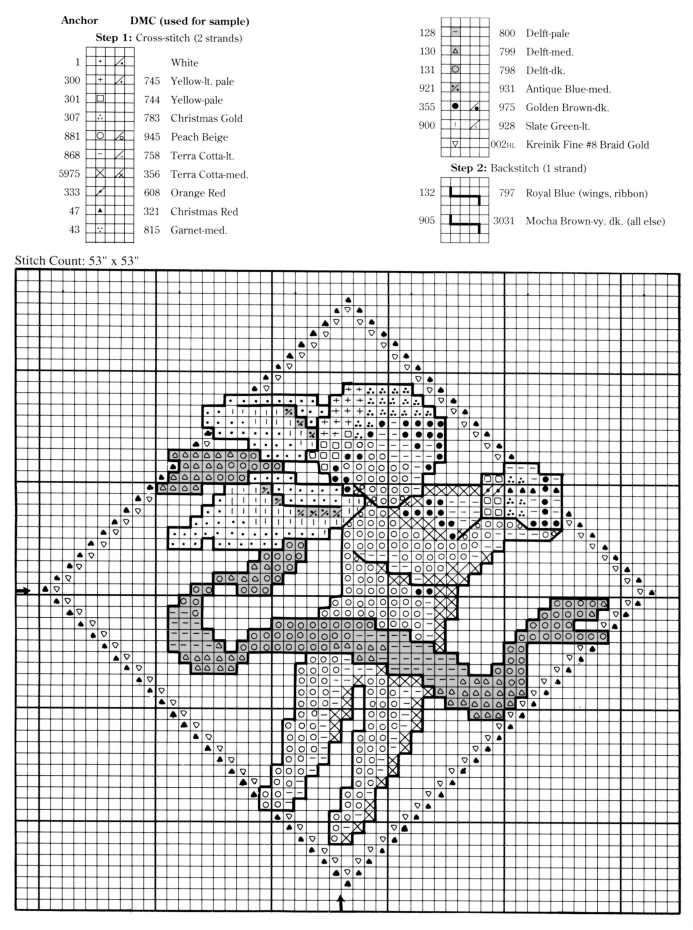

41

Angelic Coasters & Gift Tag

Stitched on emerald green Aida 14 over one thread, the finished design size is 3¾" x 3¾". The fabric was cut 6" x 6".

Stitched on ecru perforated plastic 14 over one thread, the finished design size is 2¾" x 2⅞". The paper was cut 6" x 6".

FABRICS	DESIGN SIZES
Aida 11	4¾" x 4¾"
Aida 14	3¾" x 3¾"
Aida 18	3" x 3"
Hardanger 22	2⅜" x 2⅜"

FABRICS	DESIGN SIZES
Aida 11	3½" x 3¾"
Aida 14	2¾" x 2⅞"
Aida 18	2⅛" x 2¼"
Hardanger 22	1¾" x 1⅞"

Materials (for one coaster)
Completed design on emerald green Aida 14
3½"-square acrylic coaster kit
3" square of fleece
Glue

Directions
1. Center fleece over sticky side of self-adhesive board (included in coaster kit); trim.

2. Center fleece/board over wrong side of design. Pulling snugly, wrap and glue edges to board back.

3. Insert design piece into coaster.

4. Peel protective cover from felt-covered board (included in kit). Center board over base of coaster and press in place.

Materials
Completed design on ecru perforated plastic 14
8" of ⅛"-wide metallic gold grosgrain ribbon
Yellow sewing thread
One small gold ribbon rose
Small sharp-pointed scissors

Directions
1. Trim perforated plastic one "thread" from design with sharp point of scissors.

2. Fold ⅛" gold ribbon in half to form a loop for hanger and glue folded ends to back of design piece at center top edge. Tie ribbon ends together with an overhand knot.

3. Tack ribbon rose to knot.

Anchor			DMC (used for sample)	
Step 1: Cross-stitch (2 strands)				
1	·	⁄		White
300	+	⁄	745	Yellow-lt. pale
301	□		744	Yellow-pale
307	∴		783	Christmas Gold
881	○	⁄	945	Peach Beige
868	–	⁄	758	Terra Cotta-lt.
5975	✕	⁄	356	Terra Cotta-med.
333	⁄		608	Orange Red
47	▲		321	Christmas Red
43	∵		815	Garnet-med.

128	–		800	Delft-pale
130	△		799	Delft-med.
131	○		798	Delft-dk.
921	⁒		931	Antique Blue-med.
355	●	⁄	975	Golden Brown-dk.
900	I		928	Slate Green-lt.
	▽		002HL	Kreinik Fine #8 Braid Gold

Step 2: Backstitch (1 strand)

132		797	Royal Blue (wings, ribbon)
905		3031	Mocha Brown-vy. dk. (all else)

Stitch Count: 53" x 53"

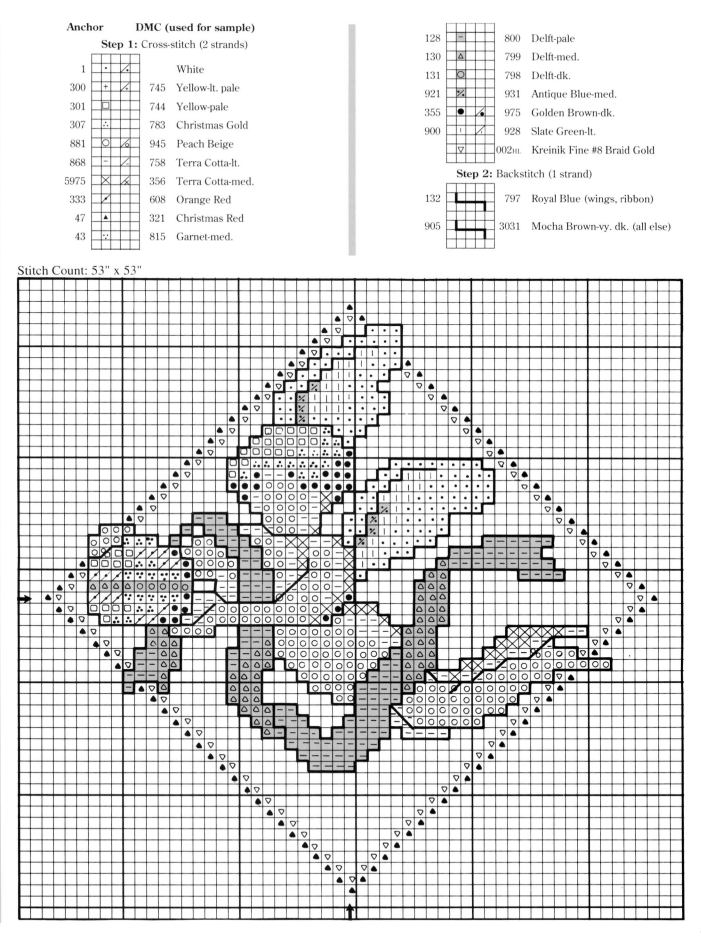

Special moments & special gifts at this holiday season will lighten & brighten for a lifetime.

PERSONALIZING BALLERINA BUNNIES

Stitched on pink Aida 18 over one thread. The finished design size varies with each letter. The fabric was cut 6" x 6" for each letter.

DMC		Anchor (used for sample)
		Step 1: Cross-stitch (2 strands)
White		1 Snow White
722		323 Apricot-lt.
3340		329 Melon-med.
963		23 Carnation-vy., vy. lt.

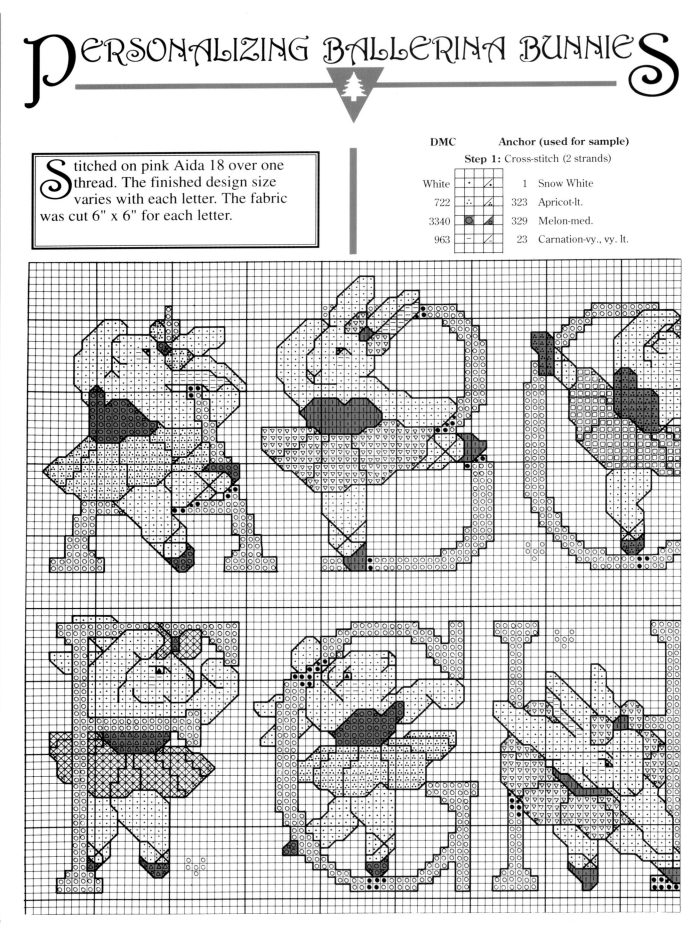

3326	☒	◩	25	Carnation-lt..
893	△	◪	27	Carnation-med.
666	○	◔	46	Crimson
321	●	⬙	47	Carmine
211	△	◭	108	Lavender-lt.
208	■	◪	110	Lavender-med.
800	╱	◨	128	Cobalt Blue-lt..
799	☒	◪	130	Cobalt Blue-med. lt.
964	▽	⬕	185	Sea Green-lt.
958	▮	◪	187	Sea Green-med.
3348	☐	◱	265	Avocado-lt.
905	▦	◪	257	Parrot Green
317	▲	◪	400	Gray-dk.

Step 2: Backstitch (1 strand)

900		333	Blaze-med. (orange outfit)
891		29	Carnation-dk. (pink outfit)
321		47	Carmine (letters)
552		112	Lavender-dk. (purple outfit)
798		131	Cobalt Blue-med. (blue outfit)
991		189	Sea Green-dk. (turquoise outfit)
987		244	Grass Green-med. dk. (green outfit)
414		235	Gray-med. (bunnies)

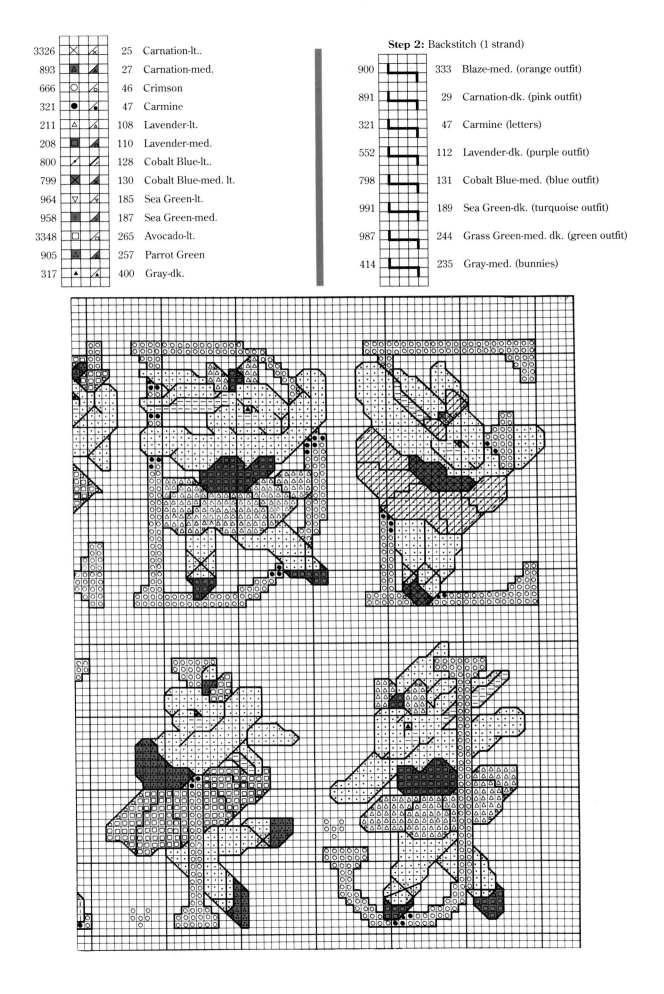

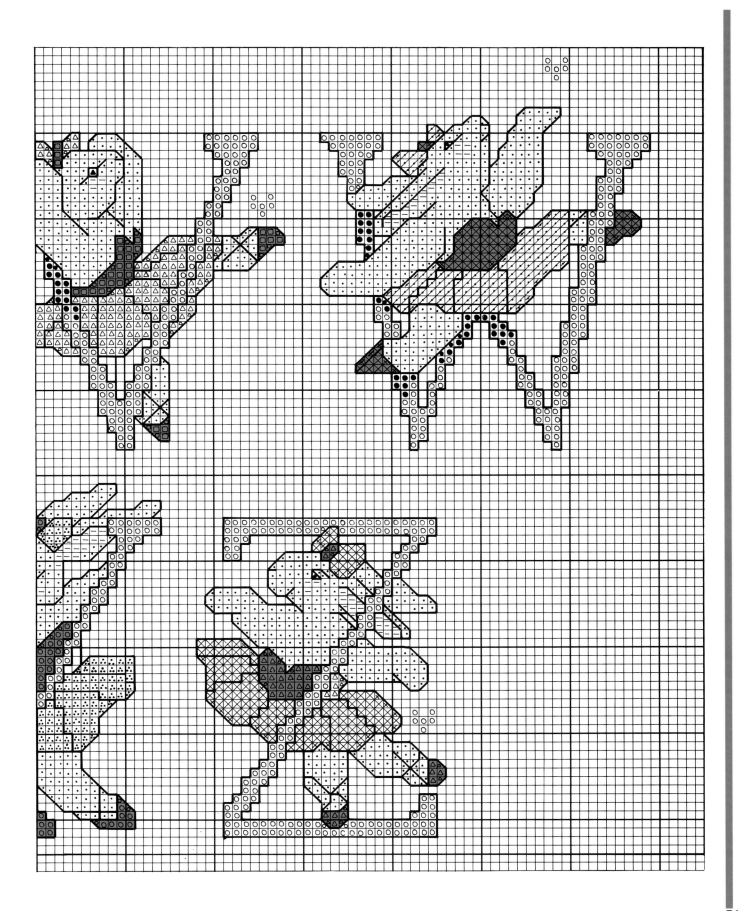

BALLERINA BUNNY ORNAMENTS

Stitched on red Aida 14 over one thread, the finished design size is 2⅛" x 3" for the green bunny, 2⅛" x 2¾" for the blue bunny, and 1⅞" x 2⅜" for the turquoise bunny. The fabric was cut 9" x 9".

BLUE BUNNY

FABRICS	DESIGN SIZES
Aida 11	2⅝" x 3½"
Aida 18	1⅝" x 2⅛"
Hardanger 22	1⅜" x 1¾"

GREEN BUNNY

FABRICS	DESIGN SIZES
Aida 11	2⅝" x 3⅞"
Aida 18	1⅝" x 2⅜"
Hardanger 22	1⅜" x 1⅞"

TURQUOISE BUNNY

FABRICS	DESIGN SIZES
Aida 11	2½" x 3⅛"
Aida 18	1½" x 1⅞"
Hardanger 22	1¼" x 1½"

MATERIALS *(for one ornament)*

Completed design (bunny only) on red Aida 14
⅛ yard of pink tulle
4" square of red fabric
3" x 4" piece of heavyweight cardboard
3" x 4" piece of lightweight cardboard
3" x 4" piece of fleece
18" of ¼"-wide pink satin ribbon
18" of ⅟₁₆"-wide satin ribbon (color to match tutu)
½"-tall ballerina shoe button
Pink sewing thread
Fabric glue stick
Glue
Tracing paper

DIRECTIONS

1. Trace and cut out ornament pattern on page 53. From heavyweight cardboard, cut one ornament. From lightweight cardboard, cut one ornament. From fleece, cut one ornament. From red fabric, cut one ornament, adding 1" to all edges. With design piece centered, cut one ornament, adding 1" to all edges. From tulle, cut one 4" x 21" strip.

2. Lightly glue fleece to heavyweight cardboard.

3. Center fleece/cardboard over wrong side of design. Pulling snugly, wrap and glue edges to cardboard back.

4. Center lightweight cardboard over wrong side of red fabric. Pulling snugly, wrap and glue edges to cardboard back.

5. With right sides facing, sew short sides of tulle strip together, making a loop. Press seam open.

6. Double-fold strip in half lengthwise and press. Sew two rows of gathering stitches ⅛" from edges. Gather to fit perimeter of design/cardboard piece. Glue gathered edge of ruffle to edge of cardboard back of design piece, allowing ⅝" of ruffle to extend beyond design piece.

7. Using glue stick, glue ⅟₁₆"-wide ribbon down center of ¼"-wide pink ribbon.

8. Fold ribbon in half, forming a loop with ⅟₁₆"-wide ribbon showing on top; glue raw ends to back of design/cardboard at center top edge.

9. Glue wrong sides of design/cardboard and fabric/cardboard together. Weight with brick or book until glue is dry.

10. Tack button to bottom center of ruffle.

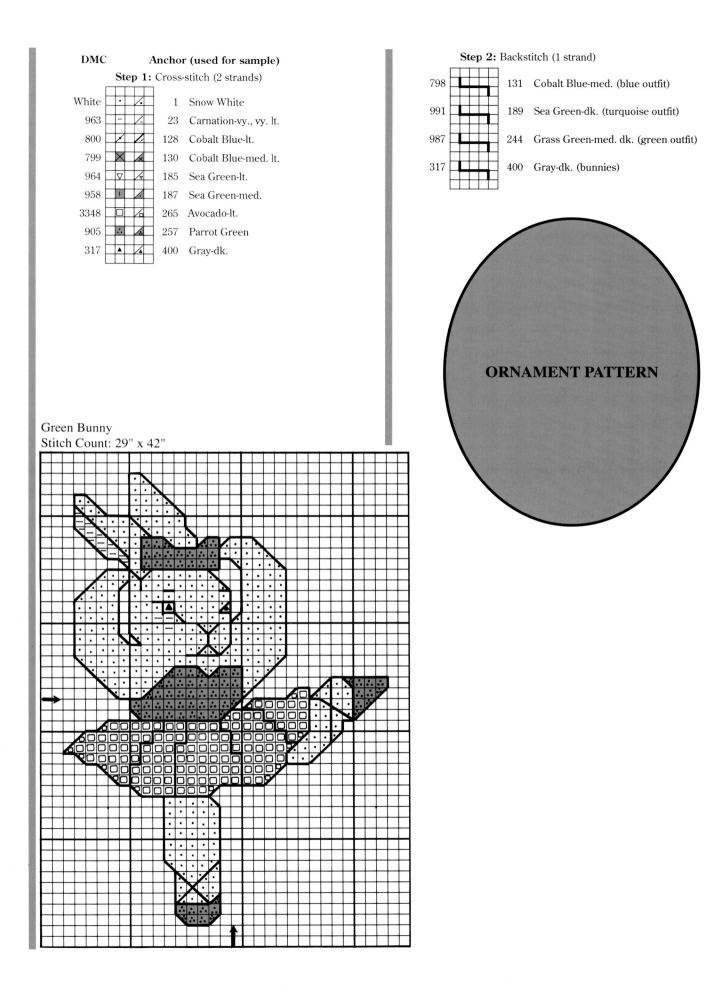

DMC	Anchor (used for sample)		
Step 1: Cross-stitch (2 strands)			
White		1	Snow White
963		23	Carnation-vy., vy. lt.
800		128	Cobalt Blue-lt.
799		130	Cobalt Blue-med. lt.
964		185	Sea Green-lt.
958		187	Sea Green-med.
3348		265	Avocado-lt.
905		257	Parrot Green
317		400	Gray-dk.

	Step 2: Backstitch (1 strand)		
798		131	Cobalt Blue-med. (blue outfit)
991		189	Sea Green-dk. (turquoise outfit)
987		244	Grass Green-med. dk. (green outfit)
317		400	Gray-dk. (bunnies)

ORNAMENT PATTERN

Green Bunny
Stitch Count: 29" x 42"

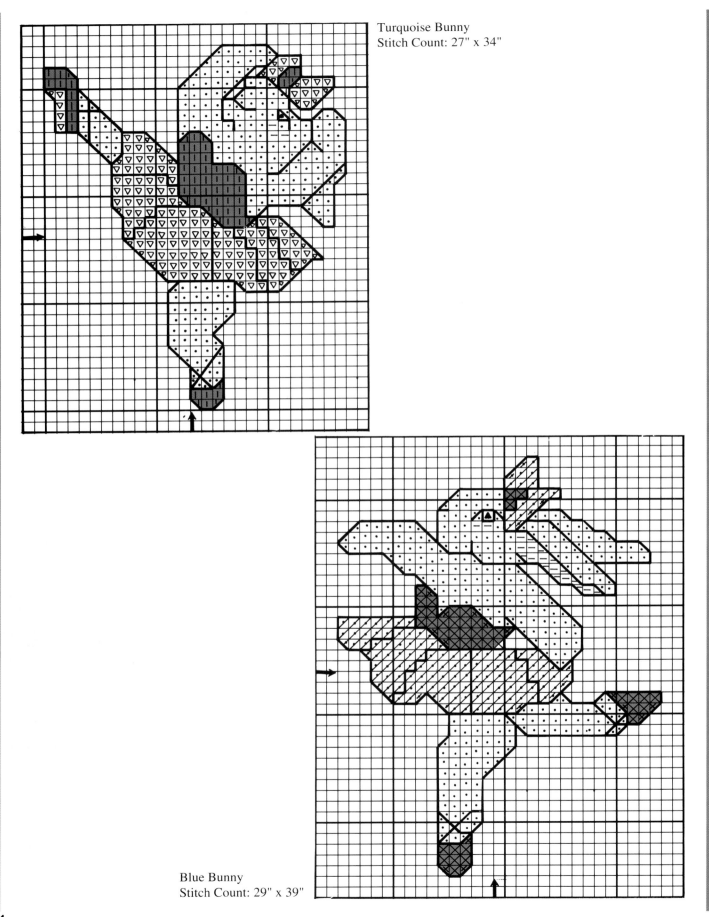

Turquoise Bunny
Stitch Count: 27" x 34"

Blue Bunny
Stitch Count: 29" x 39"

54

BALLERINA BUNNY SHIRT & TOWEL

Stitched on waste canvas 8.5 over one thread, the finished design size is 4⅝" x 5½". The fabric was cut 11" x 12".

Stitched on a premade pink hand towel with a 10" x 2½" Aida 14 inset over one thread. The finished design size is 10⅞" x 2½".

FABRICS   **DESIGN SIZES**
Aida 11   3⅜" x 4¼"
Aida 14   2⅝" x 3⅜"
Aida 18   2" x 2⅝"
Hardanger 22   1⅝" x 2⅛"

MATERIALS
7" square of waste canvas 8.5
Pink sweatshirt (child size)

DIRECTIONS
1. Center waste canvas horizontally and directly below crew-neck stitching line; baste.

2. Using six strands of floss for cross-stitch, stitch letter of choice centered horizontally and 2⅛" from top edge of waste canvas.

3. Stitch a small heart (see graph) where desired.

FABRICS   **DESIGN SIZES**
Aida 11   13⅞" x 2¾"
Aida 18   8½" x 1⅝"
Hardanger 22   6⅞" x 1⅜"

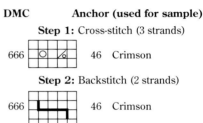

DMC	Anchor (used for sample)		
Step 1: Cross-stitch (3 strands)			
666		46	Crimson
Step 2: Backstitch (2 strands)			
666		46	Crimson

Stitch Count: 152" x 30"

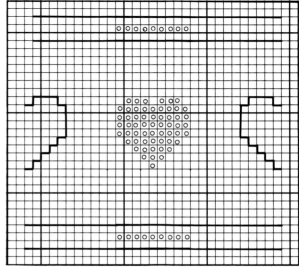

55

The stockings were hung by the chimney with care.

CHRISTMAS NUTCRACKER ORNAMENT

Stitched on white Aida 14 over one thread, the finished design size is 1¾" x 4⅛". The fabric was cut 5" x 7".

FABRICS	**DESIGN SIZES**
Aida 11	2¼" x 5⅛"
Aida 18	1⅜" x 3⅛"
Hardanger 22	1⅛" x 2⅝"

MATERIALS *(for one ornament)*
Completed design on white Aida 14
⅛ yard of red fabric; matching thread
4" x 6½" piece of fleece
18" of ⅛"-wide green grosgrain ribbon

DIRECTIONS
All seams are ½".

1. From red fabric, cut two 1⅛" x 4" strips, two 1⅛" x 6½" strips, and one 4" x 6½" piece for back. Trim design piece to 1" beyond last row of stitching on all sides.

2. With right sides facing, sew shorter strips to top and bottom of design piece. Press seams away from design. With right sides facing, sew longer strips to sides of design piece. Press seams away from design.

3. Cut a 6" length of ribbon. With raw edges aligned, tack ends to front of design piece at top edge ⅝" in from each side.

4. Baste fleece to wrong side of design piece.

5. With right sides facing, sew design/fleece front and back together, catching hanger ends in seam and leaving a 2" opening on bottom seam. Trim seams and turn. Slipstitch opening closed.

6. Machine-stitch on seam between red border and design fabric.

7. Cut remaining ribbon in half. Tie each length into a small bow. Tack bows on front below hanger ribbon; trim ribbon tails as desired.

CAROUSEL & NUTCRACKER STOCKINGS

Stitched on ivory Aida 14 for Carousel cuff, white Aida 14 for Nutcracker cuff over one thread, the finished design size is 7⅞" x 4⅜" for Carousel cuff, 8⅛" x 4⅛" for Nutcracker cuff. The fabric was cut 12" x 9".

CAROUSEL CUFF

FABRICS	DESIGN SIZES
Aida 11	10⅛" x 5½"
Aida 18	6⅛" x 3⅜"
Hardanger 22	5" x 2¾"

NUTCRACKER CUFF

FABRICS	DESIGN SIZES
Aida 11	10⅜" x 5¼"
Aida 18	6⅜" x 3¼"
Hardanger 22	5⅛" x 2⅝"

MATERIALS *(for one stocking)*
Completed design on ivory Aida 14 (Carousel) or
    white Aida 14 (Nutcracker)
1 yard of red print fabric (Carousel) or green print
    fabric (Nutcracker); matching thread
½ yard of green fabric (Carousel) or red fabric
    (Nutcracker)
⅜ yard of fleece
1½ yards of ⅛"-diameter cotton cord
1"-diameter brass ring
Tracing paper

DIRECTIONS
All seams are ½".

1. Enlarge the pattern on the grid on page 62 to make a full-size pattern. Cut out. From print fabric, cut two stockings for front and back and two for lining pieces; cut one 2" x 5" piece for hanger. From fleece, cut one stocking front. With design piece centered, trim to 9" x 6". From plain fabric, cut 1½"-wide bias strips, piecing as needed, to equal 60".

2. With right sides facing, sew bottom edge of design piece to top edge of stocking front. Press open.

3. Baste fleece to wrong side of stocking front.

4. Make piping, using cotton cord and 1½"-wide bias strips.

5. With raw edges aligned, stitch the piping down the side, around the bottom, and up the other side of the stocking front. With right sides together, stitch the stocking front to the back, sewing along the stitching line of the piping. Leave the top edge open. Trim seams; turn.

6. With right sides facing and edges aligned, stitch the lining front and back together, leaving the top edge open and an opening in the side seam above the heel. Do not turn.

7. To make hanger, fold 2" x 5" piece in half lengthwise, with right sides facing and long edges aligned. Stitch long edges. Turn. With seam at back center, fold hanger in half. Press. With raw edges matching, pin the loop adjacent to the top left side seam of the stocking.

8. Slide the lining over the stocking, right sides together. Stitch around the top edge of the stocking, securing the hanger. Turn the stocking right side out through the side opening in the lining. Slipstitch the opening closed. Slide the lining inside the stocking.

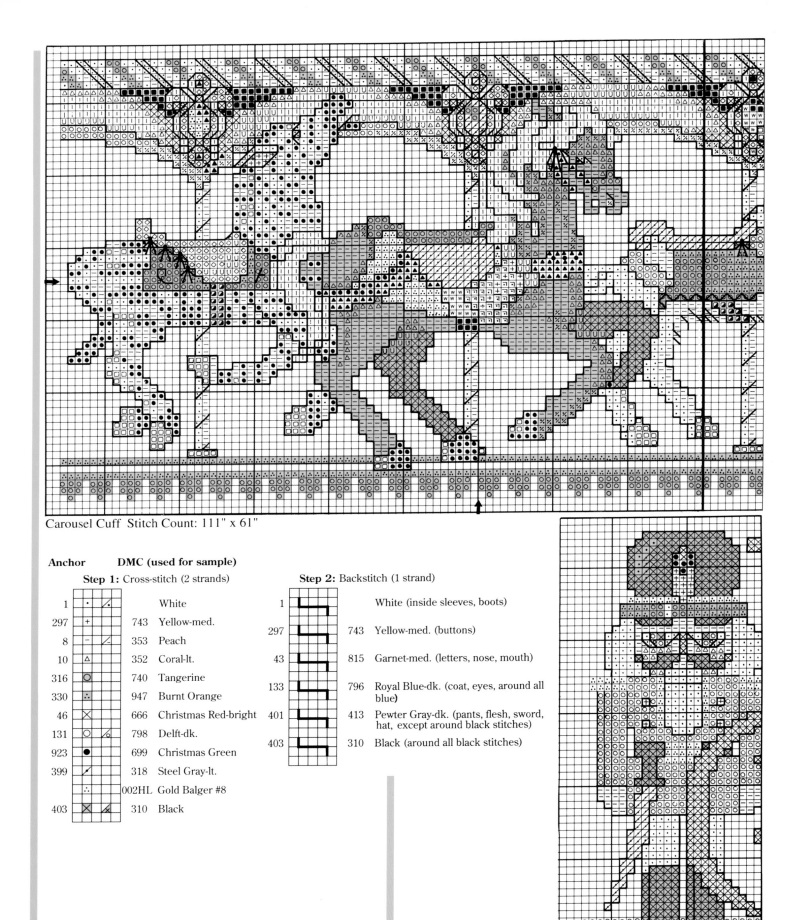

Carousel Cuff Stitch Count: 111" x 61"

Anchor		DMC (used for sample)	
Step 1: Cross-stitch (2 strands)			
1	· /		White
297	+	743	Yellow-med.
8	− /	353	Peach
10	△	352	Coral-lt.
316	⊙	740	Tangerine
330	∴	947	Burnt Orange
46	✕	666	Christmas Red-bright
131	○ ◢	798	Delft-dk.
923	●	699	Christmas Green
399	╱	318	Steel Gray-lt.
	∴	002HL	Gold Balger #8
403	✕ ◣	310	Black

Step 2: Backstitch (1 strand)			
1			White (inside sleeves, boots)
297		743	Yellow-med. (buttons)
43		815	Garnet-med. (letters, nose, mouth)
133		796	Royal Blue-dk. (coat, eyes, around all blue)
401		413	Pewter Gray-dk. (pants, flesh, sword, hat, except around black stitches)
403		310	Black (around all black stitches)

60

Anchor   **DMC (used for sample)**

Step 1: Cross-stitch (2 strands)

Anchor		DMC	
1	·		White
300	I	745	Yellow-lt. pale
297	◇	743	Yellow-med.
303	U	742	Tangerine-lt.
330	◪	947	Burnt Orange
49	◙	963	Wild Rose-vy. lt.
75	+	604	Cranberry-lt.
335	○	606	Orange Red-bright
47	∴	304	Christmas Red-med.
86	╱	3608	Plum-vy. lt.
160	○	3761	Sky Blue-lt.
167	╱	3766	Peacock Blue-lt.
433	∴	996	Electric Blue-med.
132	▲	797	Royal Blue
239	W	702	Kelly Green
228	■	910	Emerald Green-dk.
347	–	402	Mahogany-vy. lt.
324	△	922	Copper-lt.
349	╱	301	Mahogany-med.
307	△	977	Golden Brown-lt.
308	⨯	976	Golden Brown-med.
379	⨉	840	Beige Brown-med.
380	U	839	Beige Brown-dk.
398	–	415	Pearl Gray
400	□	317	Pewter Gray
403	●	310	Black

Step 2: Long Loose Stitch (1 strand)

335	╱	606	Orange Red-bright (inside canopy top)
47	╱	304	Christmas Red-med. (inside canopy top)
400	╱	317	Pewter Gray (on poles)
		002P	Gold Balger Cable (tassels on animals)

Step 3: Backstitch (1 strand)

47	⌐	304	Christmas Red-med. (red areas on animals, center pole top, zebra's mouth, bottom edge of canopy)
132	⌐	797	Royal Blue (left pole top, bridle on horse)
923	⌐	699	Christmas Green (right pole top, green areas on horse and canopy)
349	⌐	301	Mahogany-med. (around yellow on pole tops, saddle on zebra, mahogany areas on horse)
403	⌐	310	Black (eyes of animals, black areas of hooves on horse)
	⌐	002P	Gold Balger Cable (on zebra saddle, black strip on horse)
400	⌐	317	Pewter Gray (all else)

Step 4: French Knot (1 strand)

●	002P	Gold Balger Cable (tassels on animals)

Nutcracker Cuff Stitch Count: 114" x 58"

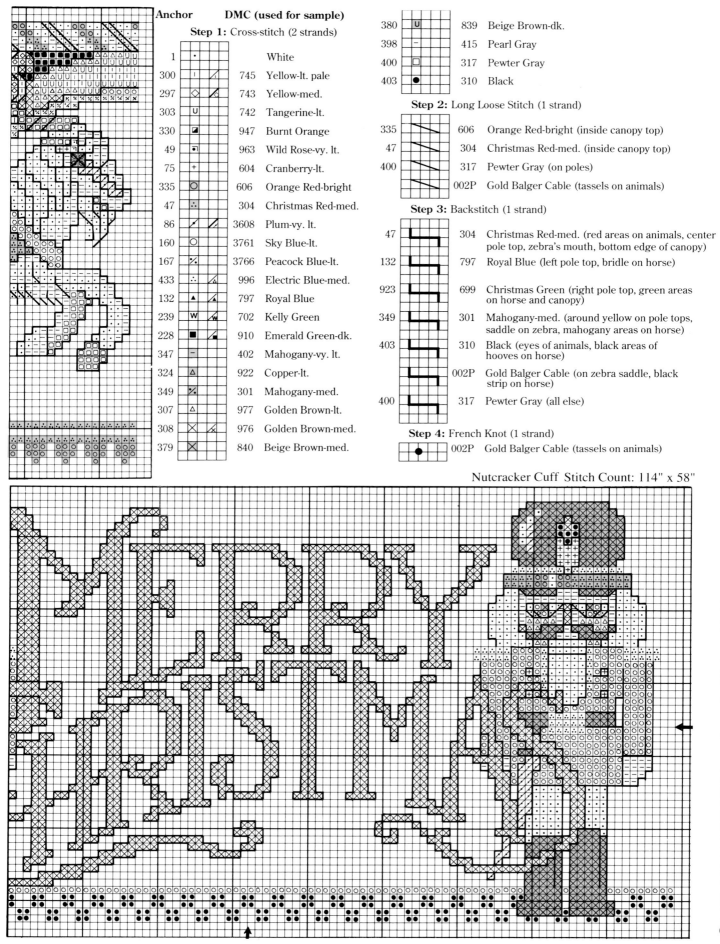

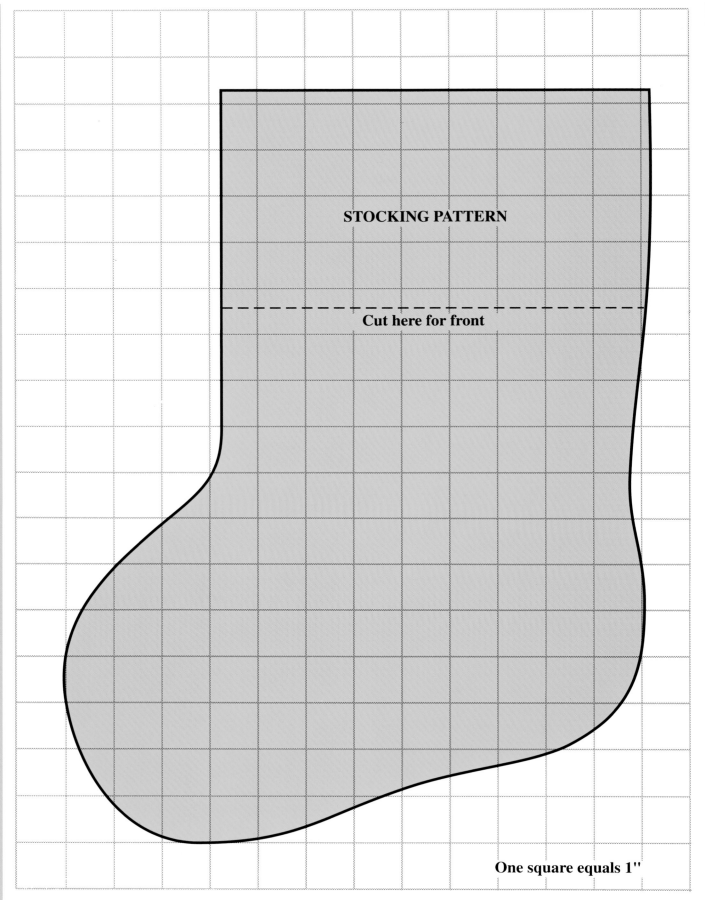

STOCKING PATTERN

Cut here for front

One square equals 1"

CHRISTMAS APRON

Stitched on a premade red-and-green tartan plaid apron with a 10" x 7" bib inset of beige Tula 10 over one thread, the finished design size is 8¾" x 5¼".

FABRICS	DESIGN SIZES
Aida 11	7⅞" x 4¾"
Aida 14	6¼" x 3¾"
Aida 18	4⅞" x 2⅞"
Hardanger 22	4" x 2⅜"

CHRISTMAS GEESE MITTEN

Stitched on natural Linen 28 over two threads, the finished design size is 8" x 4⅛". The fabric was cut 11" x 9".

FABRICS / DESIGN SIZES

FABRICS	DESIGN SIZES
Aida 11	10⅛" x 5⅛"
Aida 14	8" x 4⅛"
Aida 18	6¼" x 3⅛"
Hardanger 22	5⅛" x 2⅝"

MATERIALS

Completed design on natural Linen 28
½ yard of lightweight red/green plaid wool fabric
½ yard of green fabric for lining; matching thread
¼ yard of light tan fabric for cuff lining
⅜ yard of fleece
Tracing paper

DIRECTIONS

All seams are ½".

1. Enlarge the pattern on the grid on page 67 to make a full-size pattern. Cut out. From red/green plaid wool fabric, cut two mittens for front and back, aligning plaid pattern; cut one 2" x 5" piece for hanger. From green fabric, cut two mittens for lining front and back. From fleece, cut one mitten front. With design piece centered, trim to 9" x 6". From light tan fabric, cut one 9" x 6" piece for cuff lining.

2. With right sides facing, sew design piece to cuff lining along bottom seam only. With wrong sides facing, press.

3. Pin fleece to back of mitten front; pin design/cuff piece to mitten front, aligning top edges. Baste all layers together along top and side edges.

4. With right sides facing and edges aligned, stitch the mitten front and back together, leaving the top edge open. Trim seams; turn.

5. With right sides facing and edges aligned, stitch the lining front and back together, leaving the top edge open and an opening in the side seam above the heel. Do not turn.

6. To make hanger, fold 2" x 5" piece in half lengthwise, with right sides facing and long edges aligned. Stitch long edges. Turn. With seam at back center, fold hanger in half. Press. With raw edges matching, pin the loop adjacent to the top left side seam of the mitten.

7. Slide the lining over the mitten, right sides together. Stitch around the top edge of the mitten, securing the hanger. Turn the mitten right-side out through the side opening in the lining. Slipstitch the opening closed. Slide the lining inside the mitten.

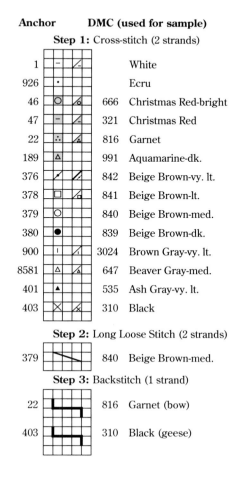

Anchor		DMC (used for sample)	
Step 1: Cross-stitch (2 strands)			
1		White	
926		Ecru	
46		666	Christmas Red-bright
47		321	Christmas Red
22		816	Garnet
189		991	Aquamarine-dk.
376		842	Beige Brown-vy. lt.
378		841	Beige Brown-lt.
379		840	Beige Brown-med.
380		839	Beige Brown-dk.
900		3024	Brown Gray-vy. lt.
8581		647	Beaver Gray-med.
401		535	Ash Gray-vy. lt.
403		310	Black
Step 2: Long Loose Stitch (2 strands)			
379		840	Beige Brown-med.
Step 3: Backstitch (1 strand)			
22		816	Garnet (bow)
403		310	Black (geese)

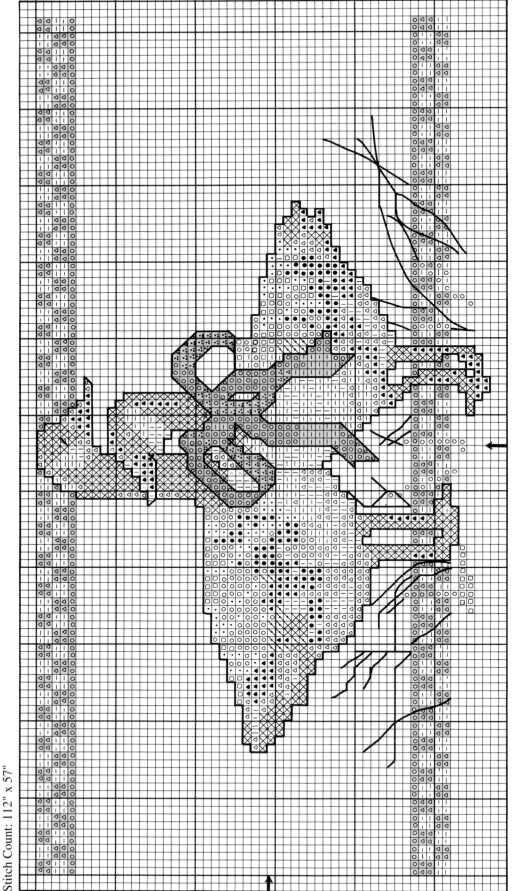

Stitch Count: 112" x 57"

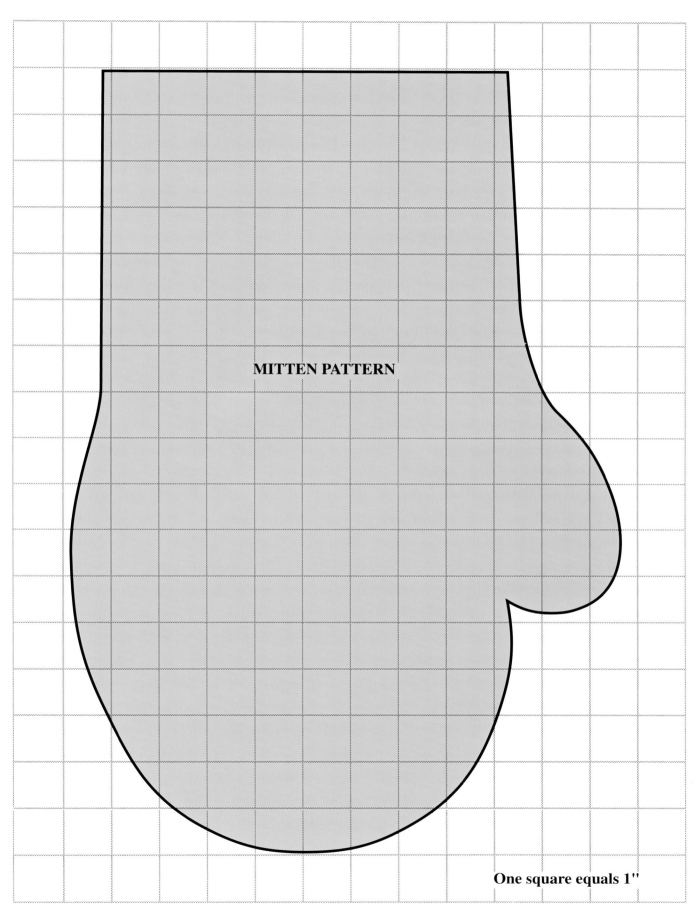

MITTEN PATTERN

One square equals 1"

CHRISTMAS GEESE BOX TOP

Stitched on natural Linen 28 over two threads, the finished design size is 5⅛" x 4⅛". The fabric was cut 9" x 9".

FABRICS	DESIGN SIZES
Aida 11	6½" x 5⅛"
Aida 14	5⅛" x 4⅛"
Aida 18	4" x 3⅛"
Hardanger 22	3¼" x 2⅝"

MATERIALS

Completed design (geese pair only) on natural Linen 28
Oak box kit with a 5¼"-square design area
8" square of tan fabric
5¾" square of fleece
5¾"-square blue-green and red mat set with a 4⅜"-square window
Glue

DIRECTIONS

1. Lightly glue fleece to cardboard. (Cardboard is included with box kit).

2. Center fleece/cardboard over wrong side of tan fabric. Pulling snugly, wrap and glue edges to cardboard back.

3. Center fabric/fleece/cardboard over wrong side of design piece. Pulling snugly, wrap and glue edges to cardboard back.

4. Glue remaining piece of cardboard (included in kit) to wrong side of design piece.

5. Insert mat set into box lid. Then, insert design piece into box lid. Secure with brads (included in kit).

The prancing & pawing of
each little hoof.

VIBRANT CAROUSEL ORNAMENTS

Stitched on red Aida 18 over one thread, the finished design size is 2⅜" x 2⅜" for each. The fabric was cut 5" x 5".

FABRICS	DESIGN SIZES
Aida 11	4" x 4"
Aida 14	3⅛" x 3⅛"
Hardanger 22	2" x 2"

MATERIALS *(for one ornament)*
Completed design on red Aida 18
4" square of red fabric
2⅞" x 3" piece of heavyweight cardboard
2⅞" x 3" piece of lightweight cardboard
2⅞" x 3" piece of fleece
14" of ³⁄₁₆"-wide twisted blue cord
3½" of 4"-wide gold fringe
5" of ⅛"-wide gold satin ribbon
Glue

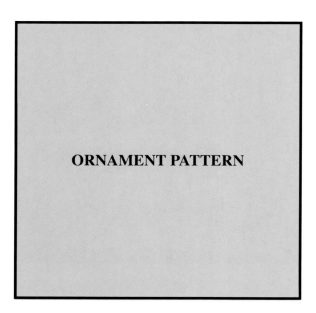

ORNAMENT PATTERN

DIRECTIONS
1. Trace and cut out ornament pattern. From heavyweight cardboard, cut one ornament. From lightweight cardboard, cut one ornament. From fleece, cut one ornament. From red fabric, cut one ornament, adding 1" to all edges. With design piece centered, cut one ornament, adding 1" to all edges.

2. Lightly glue fleece to heavyweight cardboard.

3. Center fleece/cardboard over wrong side of design. Pulling snugly, wrap and glue edges to cardboard back.

4. Center lightweight cardboard over wrong side of red fabric. Pulling snugly, wrap and glue edges to cardboard back.

5. Lightly glue cut ends on top edge of fringe to prevent raveling. Fold and glue cut ends ¼" to back; glue top ¼" of fringe to bottom edge of design-piece back.

6. Fold ⅛" gold ribbon in half to form a loop for hanger and glue raw ends to back of design/cardboard at center top edge.

7. Glue wrong sides of design/cardboard and fabric/cardboard together.

8. Glue blue cord around outside edges of ornament, covering seam. Tuck raw ends between front and back pieces. Weight with brick or book until glue is dry.

9. Trim fringe to 2½".

VIBRANT CAROUSEL AFGHAN

Stitched on royal blue Anne Cloth 18 afghan over two threads, the finished design size is 4¾" x 4¾". The fabric was cut 45" x 57".

FABRICS

FABRICS	DESIGN SIZES
Aida 11	4" x 4"
Aida 14	3⅛" x 3⅛"
Aida 18	2⅜" x 2⅜"
Hardanger 22	2" x 2"

MATERIALS
Royal blue Anne Cloth 18 afghan
Royal blue sewing thread

DIRECTIONS
1. Center and stitch carousel animals in woven squares as indicated in diagram.

2. Trim design fabric 7½" from outer woven borders on all sides; see diagram.

3. Zigzag-stitch 2" from outer woven borders on all sides.

4. Fringe all sides to zigzagged line.

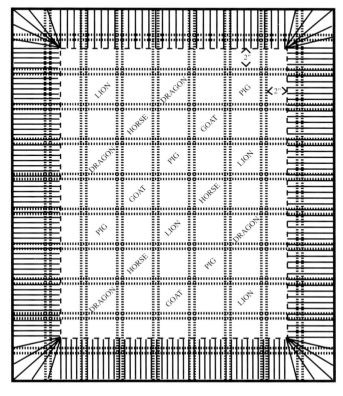

DIAGRAM

VIBRANT CAROUSEL PILLOW

Stitched on royal blue Anne Cloth 18 over two threads, the finished design size is 4¾" x 4¾". The fabric was cut 11" x 11".

FABRICS   DESIGN SIZES
Aida 11   4" x 4"
Aida 14   3⅛" x 3⅛"
Aida 18   2⅜" x 2⅜"
Hardanger 22   2" x 2"

MATERIALS
Completed design on royal blue Anne Cloth 18
½ yard of red fabric; matching thread
1¼ yards of ⅛"-diameter cotton cord
11" square of fleece
Stuffing

DIRECTIONS
1. Trim design piece 2" beyond outer woven square border on all sides. Zigzag-stitch edges to prevent fraying. Using this piece as a pattern, cut one square from red fabric for backing. Also from red fabric, cut 1½"-wide bias strips, piecing as needed, to equal 38".

2. Make piping, using cotton cord and 1½"-wide bias strips.

3. Baste fleece to back of design piece.

4. With raw edges aligned, stitch the piping around all edges of design-piece front. With right sides together, stitch the front to the back, sewing along the stitching line of the piping and leaving an opening on one side. Trim edges; turn.

5. Fill pillow moderately with stuffing. Slipstitch opening closed.

Stitch Count: 43" x 43"

Stitch Count: 43" x 43"

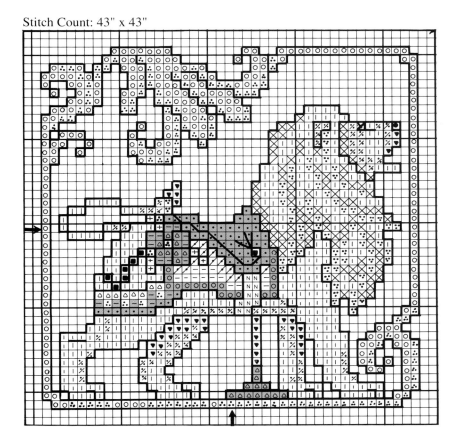

Stitch Count: 43" x 43"

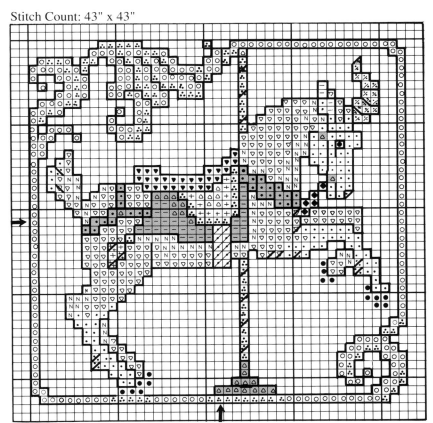

73

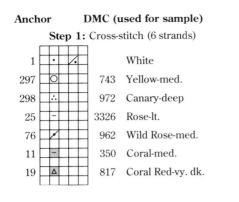

Anchor **DMC (used for sample)**

Step 1: Cross-stitch (6 strands)

1		White
297		743 Yellow-med.
298		972 Canary-deep
25		3326 Rose-lt.
76		962 Wild Rose-med.
11		350 Coral-med.
19		817 Coral Red-vy. dk.

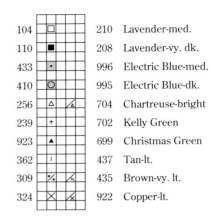

104		210 Lavender-med.
110		208 Lavender-vy. dk.
433		996 Electric Blue-med.
410		995 Electric Blue-dk.
256		704 Chartreuse-bright
239		702 Kelly Green
923		699 Christmas Green
362		437 Tan-lt.
309		435 Brown-vy. lt.
324		922 Copper-lt.

Stitch Count: 43" x 43"

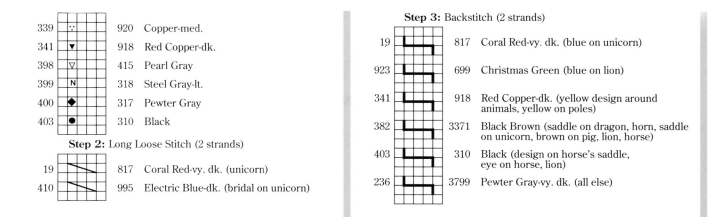

339	920	Copper-med.
341	918	Red Copper-dk.
398	415	Pearl Gray
399	318	Steel Gray-lt.
400	317	Pewter Gray
403	310	Black

Step 2: Long Loose Stitch (2 strands)

19	817	Coral Red-vy. dk. (unicorn)
410	995	Electric Blue-dk. (bridal on unicorn)

Step 3: Backstitch (2 strands)

19	817	Coral Red-vy. dk. (blue on unicorn)
923	699	Christmas Green (blue on lion)
341	918	Red Copper-dk. (yellow design around animals, yellow on poles)
382	3371	Black Brown (saddle on dragon, horn, saddle on unicorn, brown on pig, lion, horse)
403	310	Black (design on horse's saddle, eye on horse, lion)
236	3799	Pewter Gray-vy. dk. (all else)

Stitch Count: 43" x 43"

May the warm, honest snuggling of man's best friend brighten a cold, frosty day.

PERFECT PET STOCKING

Stitched on white Aida 14 over one thread, the finished design size is 6⅛" x 7⅞". The fabric was cut 13" x 14".

FABRICS	DESIGN SIZES
Aida 11	7¾" x 10"
Aida 18	4¾" x 6⅛"
Hardanger 22	3⅞" x 5"

MATERIALS
Completed design on white Aida 14
½ yard of red fabric; matching thread
1 yard of ³⁄₁₆"-diameter cotton cord
Dressmaker's pen
Tracing paper

DIRECTIONS
All seams are ½".

1. Enlarge the pattern on the grid on page 79 to make a full-size pattern. Cut out. Place the pattern on the design piece with the top edge of the pattern ¾" above and parallel to the top row of stitching. Cut out the stocking front. From red fabric, cut three stockings for back and lining; cut one 2" x 5" piece for hanger, and cut 1½"-wide bias strips, piecing as needed, to equal 36".

2. Make piping, using cotton cord and 1½"-wide bias strips.

3. With raw edges aligned, baste fleece to back of design piece.

4. With raw edges aligned, stitch the piping down the side, around the bottom, and up the other side of the design/fleece piece. With right sides together, stitch the stocking front to the back, sewing along the stitching line of the piping. Leave the top edge open. Trim seams; turn.

5. With right sides facing and edges aligned, stitch the lining front and back together, leaving the top edge open and an opening in the side seam above the heel. Do not turn.

6. To make hanger, fold 2" x 5" piece in half lengthwise, with right sides facing and long edges aligned. Stitch long edges. Turn. With seam at back center, fold hanger in half. Press. With raw edges matching, pin the hanger to the top right side seam of the stocking.

7. Slide the lining over the stocking, right sides together. Stitch around the top edge of the stocking, securing the hanger. Turn the stocking right side out through the side opening in the lining. Slipstitch the opening closed. Slide the lining inside the stocking.

Anchor   **DMC (used for sample)**

Step 1: Cross-stitch (2 strands)

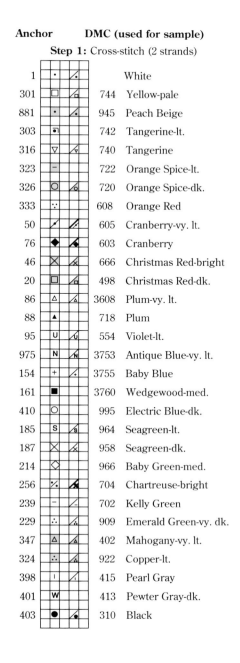

Anchor	DMC	Color
1		White
301	744	Yellow-pale
881	945	Peach Beige
303	742	Tangerine-lt.
316	740	Tangerine
323	722	Orange Spice-lt.
326	720	Orange Spice-dk.
333	608	Orange Red
50	605	Cranberry-vy. lt.
76	603	Cranberry
46	666	Christmas Red-bright
20	498	Christmas Red-dk.
86	3608	Plum-vy. lt.
88	718	Plum
95	554	Violet-lt.
975	3753	Antique Blue-vy. lt.
154	3755	Baby Blue
161	3760	Wedgewood-med.
410	995	Electric Blue-dk.
185	964	Seagreen-lt.
187	958	Seagreen-dk.
214	966	Baby Green-med.
256	704	Chartreuse-bright
239	702	Kelly Green
229	909	Emerald Green-vy. dk.
347	402	Mahogany-vy. lt.
324	922	Copper-lt.
398	415	Pearl Gray
401	413	Pewter Gray-dk.
403	310	Black

Step 2: Backstitch (1 strand)

Anchor	DMC	Color
46	666	Christmas Red-bright (bows on Christmas tree)
187	958	Seagreen-dk. (yarn)
229	909	Emerald Green-vy. dk. (carrot tops)
401	413	Pewter Gray-dk. (all else)

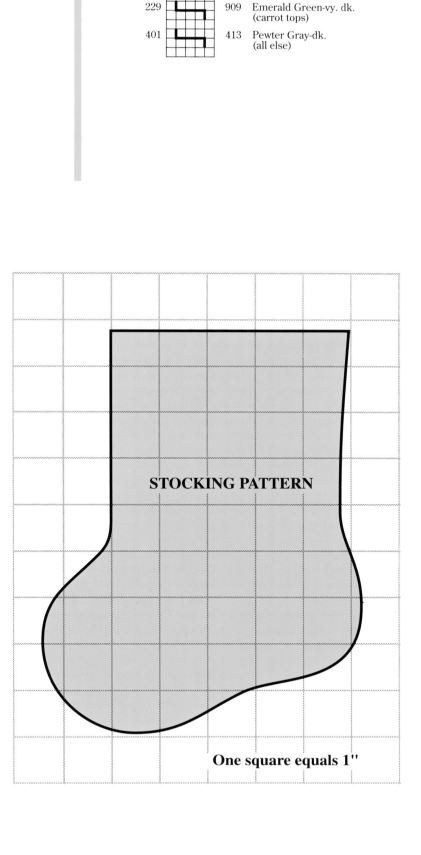

STOCKING PATTERN

One square equals 1″

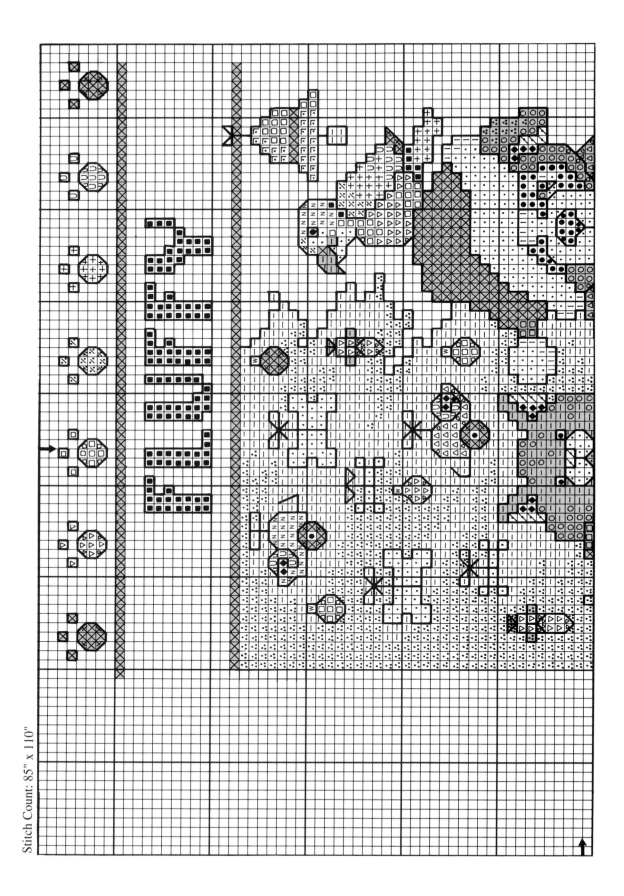

Stitch Count: 85" x 110"

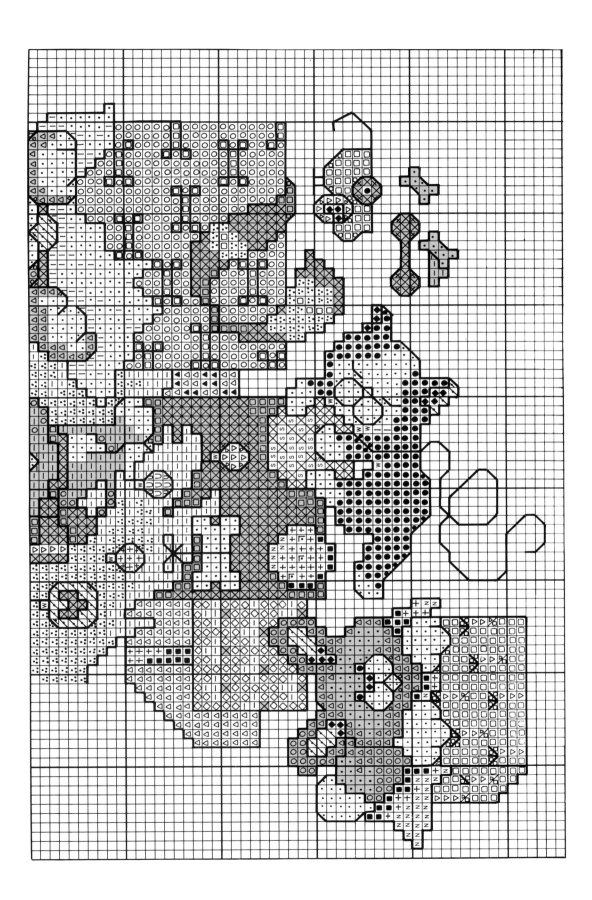

ᴘERFECT ᴘET ORNAMENTS

Stitched on white Aida 18 for dog, or white Aida 14 for bunny over one thread, the finished design size is 1⅞" x 2⅞" for the dog, 1⅞" x 1⅞" for the bunny. The fabric was cut 8" x 9" for the dog, 8" x 8" for the bunny.

DOG ORNAMENT

FABRICS	DESIGN SIZES
Aida 11	3" x 4¾"
Aida 14	2⅜" x 3¾"
Hardanger 22	1½" x 2⅜"

BUNNY ORNAMENT

FABRICS	DESIGN SIZES
Aida 11	2½" x 2½"
Aida 18	1½" x 1½"
Hardanger 22	1¼" x 1¼"

MATERIALS *(for one ornament)*
Completed design on white Aida 18 (dog),
   Aida 14 (bunny)
10" of ⅛"-wide red satin ribbon
White sewing thread
1"-tall novelty button (candy cane for dog; carrot
   for bunny)
3¾" of ³⁄₁₆"-diameter wooden dowel
Two ⅝"-diameter wooden beads
Red acrylic paint
Paintbrush
Tracing paper

DIRECTIONS
1. Trim design piece to 5½" x 6¾" with design centered horizontally and 1¾" from bottom edge for dog (1½" from bottom for bunny).

2. With right sides facing, sew long edges together. Trim seam allowance and press seam open at center back.

3. Measure and mark points 1" from bottom edge on each side and center bottom point. Lightly draw lines connecting points, forming a V; see diagram. Sew bottom seam on lines and trim seam allowance. Clip corners. Turn right side out; press.

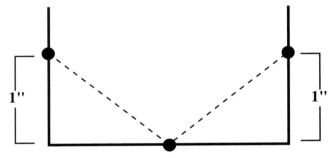

DIAGRAM

4. Zigzag-stitch raw end (for bunny, trim design piece to 5" before stitching); set aside.

5. To make hanger, insert dowel ends into beads. Paint hanger red.

6. For hanger casing, turn zigzagged edge under ¼" and slipstitch to back of ornament, sandwiching hanger in casing.

7. Tie ends of ribbon to each end of dowel. Tack button to bottom point on ornament front.

PERFECT PET TOWEL

Stitched on a purchased white hand towel with a 13" x 3" white Aida 14 inset over one thread, the finished design size is 13¼" x 1¾".

2. Center and stitch desired name two squares below red line border.

3. Stitch lower red line border two squares below name.

4. Stitch lower paw border; repeat entire upper paw border one square below lower red line.

FABRICS   DESIGN SIZES
Aida 11   16⅞" x 2¼"
Aida 18   10¼" x 1⅜"
Hardanger 22   8⅜" x 1⅛"

MATERIALS
Purchased white hand towel

DIRECTIONS
1. Starting eight squares down from top of inset, stitch upper paw border and upper red line. Extend borders to the sides of the towel.

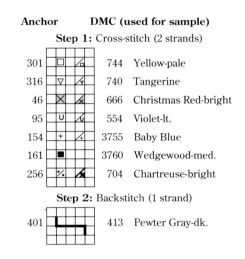

Anchor			DMC (used for sample)	
Step 1: Cross-stitch (2 strands)				
301	□	◹	744	Yellow-pale
316	▽	◸	740	Tangerine
46	✕	◪	666	Christmas Red-bright
95	U	◹	554	Violet-lt.
154	+	◿	3755	Baby Blue
161	■		3760	Wedgewood-med.
256	⁒	◸	704	Chartreuse-bright
Step 2: Backstitch (1 strand)				
401			413	Pewter Gray-dk.

Not a creature was stirring, not even a mouse.

Mouse House

Stitched on white Aida 14 over one thread, the finished design size is 7¼" x 11⅜". The fabric was cut 14" x 18".

Stitch Count: 101" x 160"

FABRICS

FABRICS	DESIGN SIZES
Aida 11	9⅛" x 14½"
Aida 18	5⅝" x 8⅞"
Hardanger 22	4⅝" x 7¼"

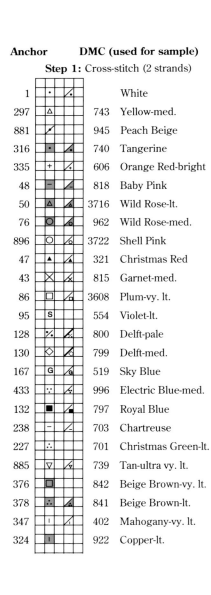

Anchor		DMC (used for sample)	
Step 1: Cross-stitch (2 strands)			
1	· ⁄		White
297	△ ⁄	743	Yellow-med.
881	⁄ ⁄	945	Peach Beige
316	▪ ⁄	740	Tangerine
335	+ ⁄	606	Orange Red-bright
48	– ⁄	818	Baby Pink
50	▲ ⁄	3716	Wild Rose-lt.
76	○ ⁄	962	Wild Rose-med.
896	○ ⁄	3722	Shell Pink
47	▲ ⁄	321	Christmas Red
43	✕ ⁄	815	Garnet-med.
86	□ ⁄	3608	Plum-vy. lt.
95	S ⁄	554	Violet-lt.
128	⁒ ⁄	800	Delft-pale
130	◇ ⁄	799	Delft-med.
167	G ⁄	519	Sky Blue
433	∴ ⁄	996	Electric Blue-med.
132	■ ■	797	Royal Blue
238	– ⁄	703	Chartreuse
227	∴	701	Christmas Green-lt.
885	▽ ⁄	739	Tan-ultra vy. lt.
376	▢ ⁄	842	Beige Brown-vy. lt.
378	∴ ⁄	841	Beige Brown-lt.
347	∣ ⁄	402	Mahogany-vy. lt.
324	∣	922	Copper-lt.

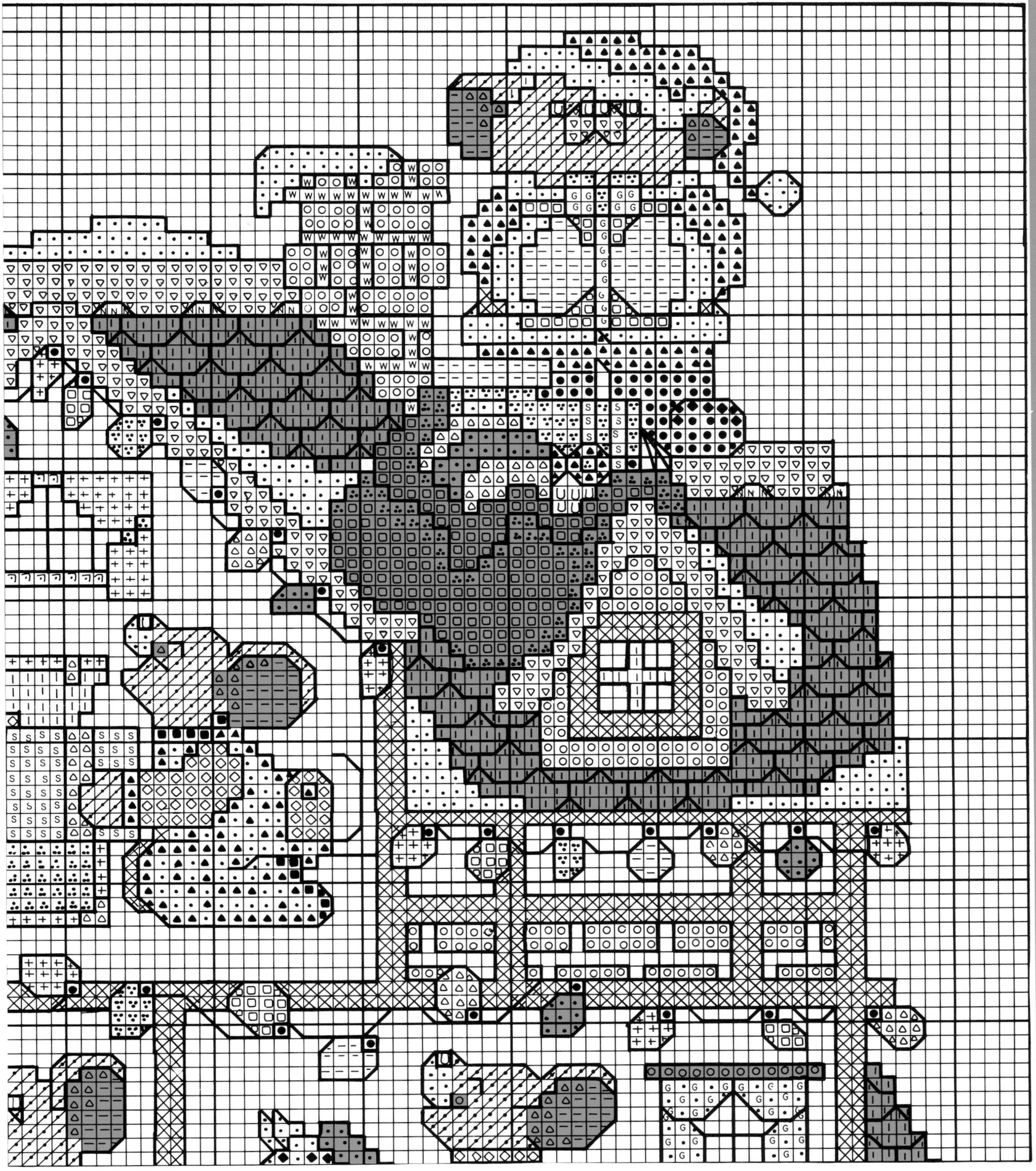

349			921	Copper
341	N		918	Red Copper-dk.
360	U		898	Coffee Brown-vy. dk.
398	W	W	415	Pearl Gray
400	◆		414	Steel Gray-dk.
401	▼		413	Pewter Gray-dk.
403	●		310	Black

Step 2: Backstitch (1 strand)

47		321	Christmas Red (reins; doll's mouth, apron, bloomers; red on mouse's sleeve, mouse's apron; berries)
227		701	Christmas Green-lt. (xmas tree, holly, wreath, letters on welcome mat)
341		918	Red Copper-dk. (roof shingles, welcome mat, garland on xmas tree, doll's hair, face)
360		898	Coffee Brown-vy. dk. (mice, Santa's sack)
401		413	Pewter Gray-dk. (all else)

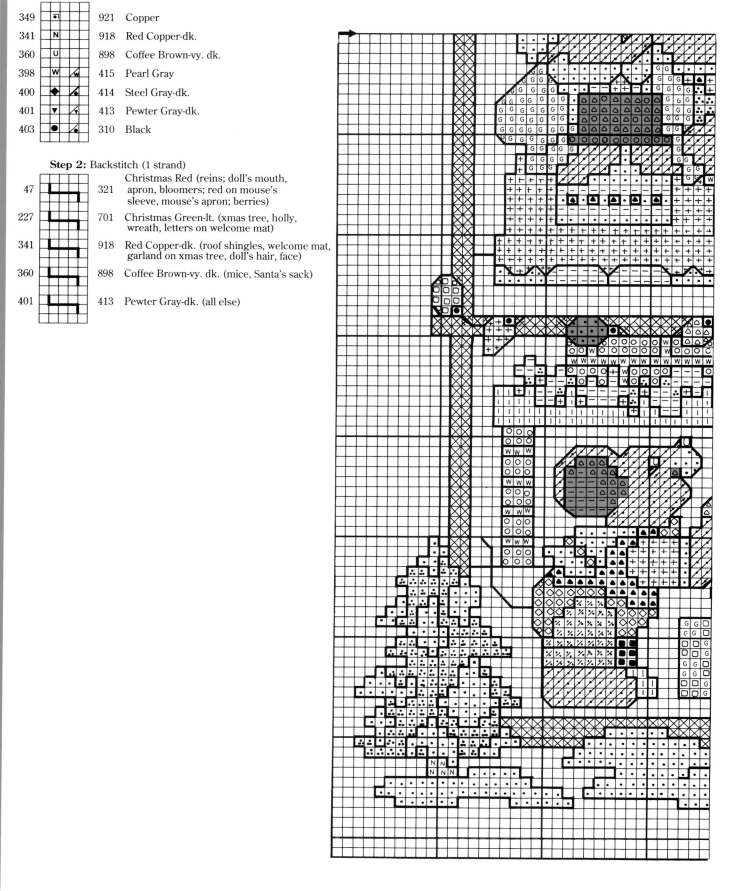

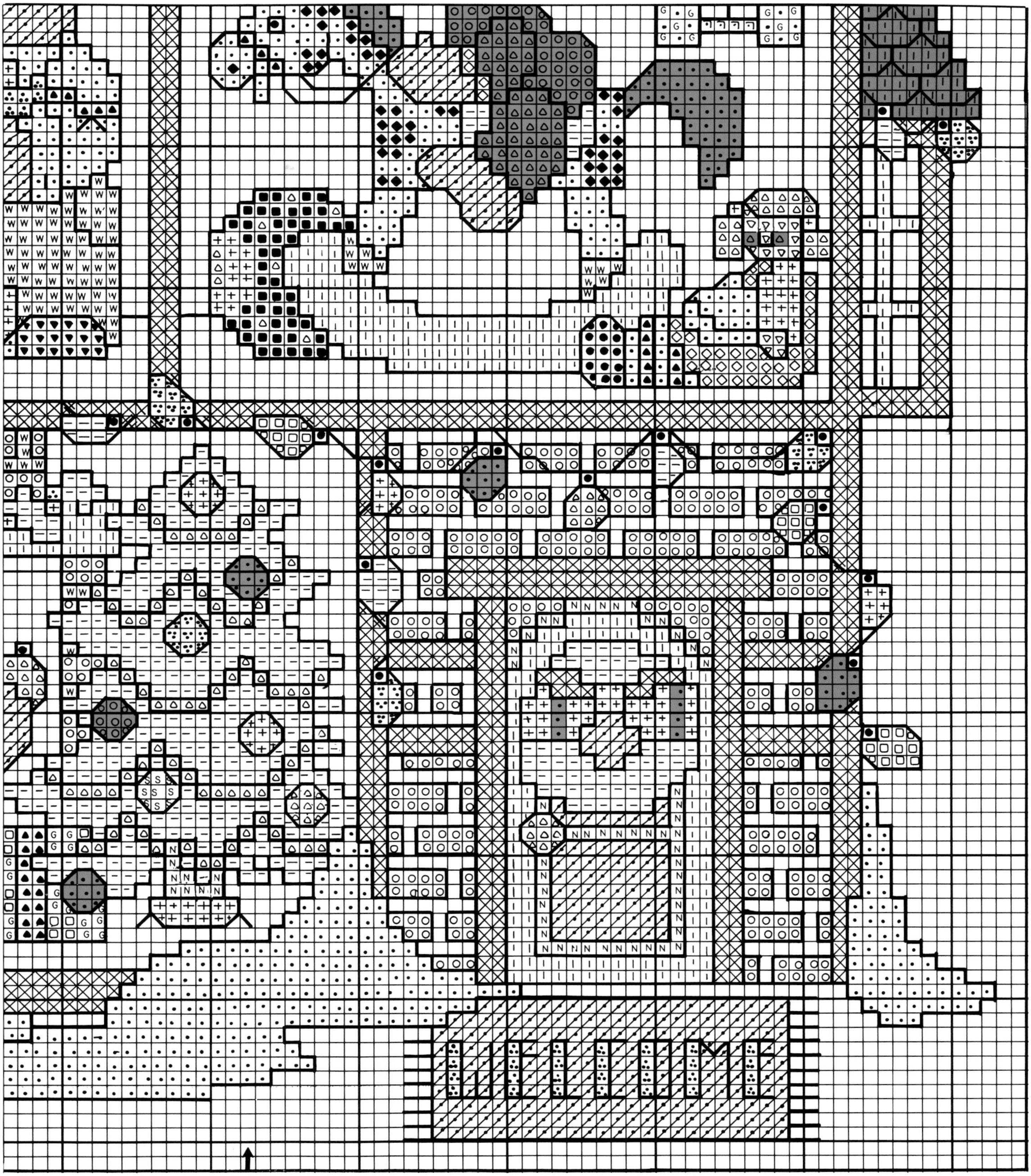

Mouse House Tote Ornament

Stitched on white Aida 18 over one thread, the finished design size is 1½" x 1⅞" for Santa, 1⅞" x 2⅛" for Mr. & Mrs. Mouse, 2¼" x 2⅛" for rocking horse, and 1⅝" x 1¾" for mouse. The fabric was cut 6" x 6".

SANTA

FABRICS	DESIGN SIZES
Aida 11	2½" x 3⅛"
Aida 14	2" x 2⅜"
Hardanger 22	1¼" x 1½"

MR. & MRS. MOUSE

FABRICS	DESIGN SIZES
Aida 11	3" x 3½"
Aida 14	2⅜" x 2¾"
Hardanger 22	1½" x 1¾"

ROCKING HORSE

FABRICS	DESIGN SIZES
Aida 11	3⅝" x 3½"
Aida 14	2⅞" x 2¾"
Hardanger 22	1⅞" x 1¾"

MOUSE

FABRICS	DESIGN SIZES
Aida 11	2⅝" x 2⅞"
Aida 14	2⅛" x 2¼"
Hardanger 22	1⅜" x 1⅜"

MATERIALS *(for one ornament)*
Completed design on white Aida 18
¼ yard of Christmas print fabric; green thread
¼ yard of red fabric
3" square of iron-on interfacing
7" of ¼"-wide red grosgrain ribbon
Red embroidery floss

DIRECTIONS
All seams are ¼".

1. From Christmas print fabric, cut one piece 8" x 10". From red fabric, cut one piece 8" x 10". Trim design piece to ⅜" beyond last row of stitching on all sides. Fringe all edges ¼". Trim interfacing to fit unfringed area of design piece.

2. Adhere interfacing to back of design fabric, following manufacturer's instructions.

3. Pin design piece to print fabric with design centered horizontally and 1¼" from top edge.

4. Using red thread, hand-sew a running stitch two squares from last row of stitching around all sides in an over-one-square, under-one-square pattern.

5. To make outer bag, trim print fabric to 1¼" beyond sides of design piece. With wrong sides facing, fold print fabric 1" from bottom of design piece; trim top edges even. Using this piece as pattern, cut one lining piece from red fabric.

6. With right sides of outer bag facing, sew each side. Repeat for lining, except leave a 1½" opening on one side. Trim seams.

7. Turn outer bag right side out and press.

8. Matching raw edges, pin ribbon ends to outer bag at each side seam.

9. Slide lining over outer bag, right sides together. Sew outer bag and lining together along top edge. Trim seams. Turn the bag right side out and slip-stitch the opening closed. Slide the lining inside the bag.

Suggested bag fillers: *greenery, small cones, small glass ball ornaments. cinnamon sticks, small wrapped packages, small stuffed toys, miniature sled or musical instruments.*

Anchor   **DMC (used for sample)**

Step 1: Cross-stitch (2 strands)

Anchor			DMC	
1				White
881			945	Peach Beige
316			740	Tangerine
48			818	Baby Pink
50			3716	Wild Rose-lt.
76			962	Wild Rose-med.
47			321	Christmas Red
43			815	Garnet-med.
86			3608	Plum-vy. lt.
130			799	Delft-med.
167			519	Sky Blue
433			996	Electric Blue-med.
238			703	Chartreuse
885			739	Tan-ultra vy. lt.
347			402	Mahogany-vy. lt.
360			898	Coffee Brown-vy. dk.
398			415	Pearl Gray
400			414	Steel Gray-dk.
403			310	Black

Step 2: Backstitch (1 strand)

		DMC	
47		321	Christmas Red (reins)
360		898	Coffee Brown-vy. dk. (mice)
401		413	Pewter Gray-dk. (all else)

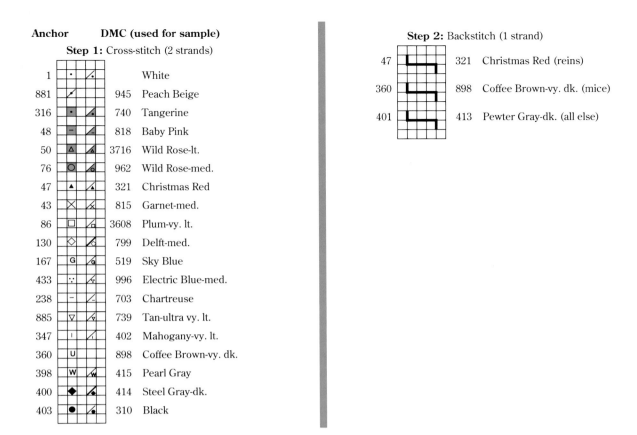

Santa
Stitch Count: 28" x 34"

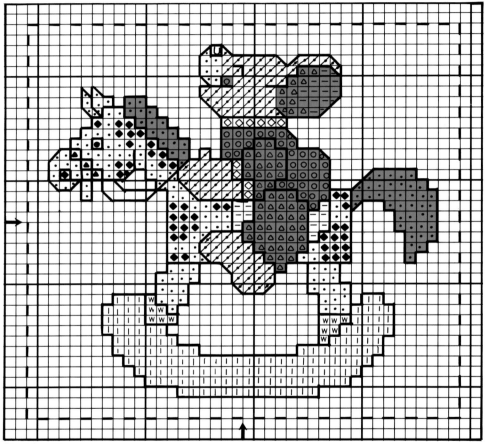

Rocking Horse
Stitch Count: 40" x 38"

May the sparkle of friends light up
your Christmas.

Mouse Tree House Pillow

Stitched on an 11" x 11" purchased pillow of 7-count fabric over one thread, the finished design size is 10¼" x 9½".

FABRICS
Aida 11
Aida 14
Aida 18
Hardanger 22

DESIGN SIZES
6½" x 6"
5⅛" x 4¾"
4" x 3⅝"
3¼" x 3"

MATERIALS
11" square premade pillow (7 count) with 2½" ruffle
12"-square pillow form

DIRECTIONS
1. Center and stitch mice design, using six strands of floss.

2. Insert pillow form into pillow.

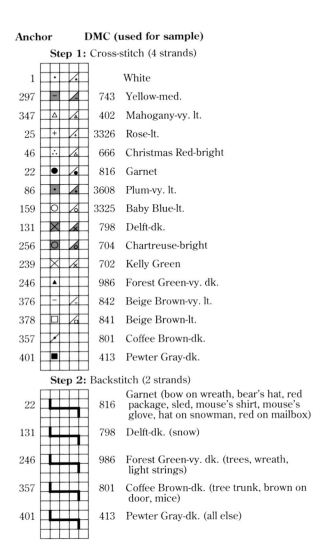

Anchor			DMC (used for sample)	
Step 1: Cross-stitch (4 strands)				
1	·	⁄		White
297	−	⁄	743	Yellow-med.
347	△	⁄	402	Mahogany-vy. lt.
25	+	⁄	3326	Rose-lt.
46	∴	⁄	666	Christmas Red-bright
22	●	⁄	816	Garnet
86	▫	⁄	3608	Plum-vy. lt.
159	○	⁄	3325	Baby Blue-lt.
131	✕	⁄	798	Delft-dk.
256	⊙	⁄	704	Chartreuse-bright
239	⊠	⁄	702	Kelly Green
246	▲		986	Forest Green-vy. dk.
376	−	⁄	842	Beige Brown-vy. lt.
378	□	⁄	841	Beige Brown-lt.
357	⁄		801	Coffee Brown-dk.
401	■		413	Pewter Gray-dk.
Step 2: Backstitch (2 strands)				
22			816	Garnet (bow on wreath, bear's hat, red package, sled, mouse's shirt, mouse's glove, hat on snowman, red on mailbox)
131			798	Delft-dk. (snow)
246			986	Forest Green-vy. dk. (trees, wreath, light strings)
357			801	Coffee Brown-dk. (tree trunk, brown on door, mice)
401			413	Pewter Gray-dk. (all else)

Stitch Count: 71" x 66"

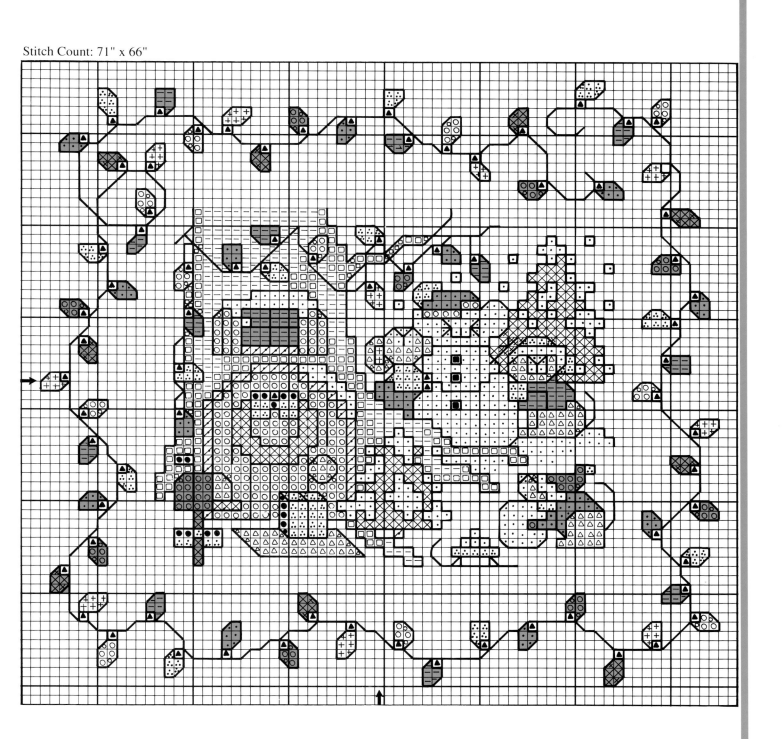

MOUSE TREE HOUSE STOCKING

Stitched on a purchased stocking with a 5¾" x 3½" ivory Aida 14 inset over one thread, the finished design size is 5⅞" x 2⅜".

FABRICS

FABRICS	DESIGN SIZES
Aida 11	7½" x 3"
Aida 18	4⅝" x 1⅞"
Hardanger 22	3¾" x 1½"

MATERIALS
Premade stocking

DIRECTIONS
1. Using three strands of floss, stitch name two squares above bottom edge of Aida inset and centered horizontally.

2. Stitch toy design two squares above name and centered horizontally.

Stitch Count: 83" x 33"

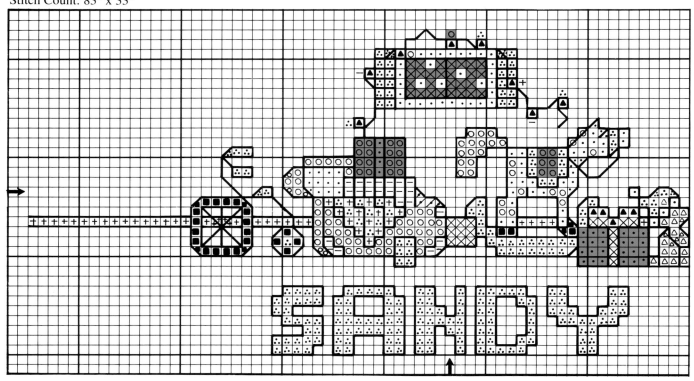

Anchor   **DMC (used for sample)**

Step 1: Cross-stitch (2 strands)

Anchor			DMC	Color
1	·	⁄		White
297	−	⁄	743	Yellow-med.
347	△	⁄	402	Mahogany-vy. lt.
25	+	⁄	3326	Rose-lt.
46	∴	⁄	666	Christmas Red-bright
86	⊡	⁄	3608	Plum-vy. lt.
159	○	⁄	3325	Baby Blue-lt.
131	✕	⁄	798	Delft-dk.
256	◉	⁄	704	Chartreuse-bright
239	⨯	⁄	702	Kelly Green
246	▲		986	Forest Green-vy. dk.
357	⁄		801	Coffee Brown-dk.
401	■		413	Pewter Gray-dk.

Step 2: Backstitch (1 strand)

Anchor		DMC	Color
22		816	Garnet (letters, bike's handles and seat, horse's saddle, rockers and reins, bear's hat, red package, lines on yellow package)
131		798	Delft-dk. (blue toy box)
246		986	Forest Green-vy. dk. (light strings, green bow, small green package on bear's lap)
357		801	Coffee Brown-dk. (bear)
401		413	Pewter Gray-dk. (all else)

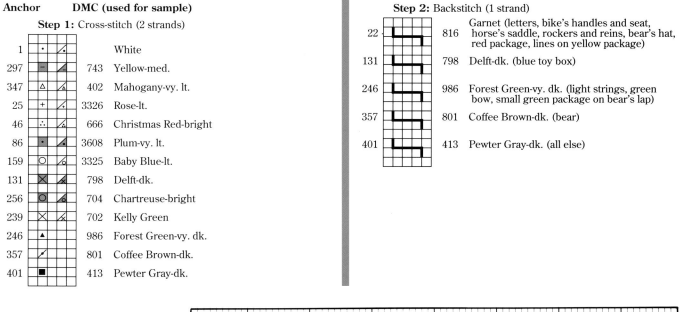

Let your dreams bring enchantment,
magic & fairy princesses to life.

ELEGANT FAIRY ORNAMENT

FABRICS / DESIGN SIZES

FABRICS	DESIGN SIZES
Aida 11	4½" x 4¾"
Aida 18	2¾" x 2⅞"
Hardanger 22	2¼" x 2⅜"

MATERIALS

Completed design on 6"-square of black Aida 14
¼ yard of purple fabric
4" square of heavyweight cardboard
4" square of lightweight cardboard
4" square of fleece
6" of ⅛"-wide purple satin ribbon
15" of ³⁄₁₆"-diameter cotton cord
One 3½"-long multicolored tassel
Glue
Tracing paper

DIRECTIONS

1. Trace and cut out ornament pattern on page 101. From heavyweight cardboard, cut one ornament. From lightweight cardboard, cut one ornament. From fleece, cut one ornament. From purple fabric, cut one ornament, adding 1" to all edges. Also from purple fabric, cut ½"-wide bias strips, piecing as needed to equal 20". With design piece centered, cut one ornament, adding 1" to all edges.

2. Lightly glue fleece to heavyweight cardboard.

3. Center fleece/cardboard over wrong side of design. Pulling snugly, wrap and glue edges to cardboard back.

4. Center lightweight cardboard over wrong side of purple fabric. Pulling snugly, wrap and glue edges to cardboard back.

5. Make piping, using cotton cord and 1½"-wide bias strips.

6. Glue piping around back edge of design/cardboard, overlapping ends at center bottom.

7. Fold ⅛" purple ribbon in half to form a loop for hanger and glue raw ends to back of design/cardboard at center top edge.

8. Attach tassel to design/cardboard at center bottom.

9. Glue wrong sides of design/cardboard and fabric/cardboard together. Weight with brick or book until glue is dry.

Stitch Count: 50" x 52"

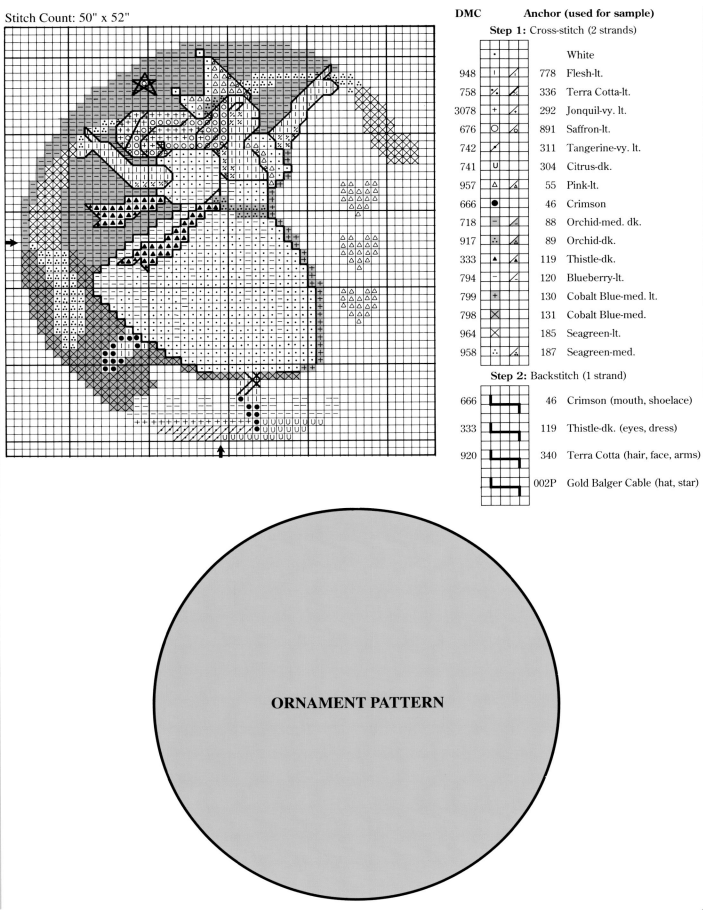

DMC			Anchor (used for sample)

Step 1: Cross-stitch (2 strands)

DMC			Anchor	
	·			White
948	I	╱	778	Flesh-lt.
758	╱.	╱	336	Terra Cotta-lt.
3078	+	╱	292	Jonquil-vy. lt.
676	O	╱	891	Saffron-lt.
742	╱		311	Tangerine-vy. lt.
741	U		304	Citrus-dk.
957	△	╱	55	Pink-lt.
666	●		46	Crimson
718	−	╱	88	Orchid-med. dk.
917	∴	╱	89	Orchid-dk.
333	▲	╱	119	Thistle-dk.
794	−	╱	120	Blueberry-lt.
799	+		130	Cobalt Blue-med. lt.
798	✕		131	Cobalt Blue-med.
964	✕		185	Seagreen-lt.
958	∴	╱	187	Seagreen-med.

Step 2: Backstitch (1 strand)

DMC		Anchor	
666		46	Crimson (mouth, shoelace)
333		119	Thistle-dk. (eyes, dress)
920		340	Terra Cotta (hair, face, arms)
		002P	Gold Balger Cable (hat, star)

ORNAMENT PATTERN

101

ELEGANT NUTCRACKER STOCKING

Stitched on black Aida 14 over one thread, the finished design size is 8⅞" x 16⅜". The fabric was cut 14" x 21".

FABRICS   **DESIGN SIZES**
Aida 11   11¼" x 20⅞"
Aida 18   6⅞" x 12¾"
Hardanger 22   5⅝" x 10⅜"

MATERIALS
Completed design on black Aida 14
½ yard of purple/blue print fabric
½ yard of purple fabric
⅜ yard of fleece
1½ yards of ³⁄₁₆"-diameter cotton cord
Black sewing thread
Tracing paper

DIRECTIONS
All seams are ½".

1. Enlarge the pattern on the grid on page 103 to make a full-size pattern. Cut out. From design piece, cut one stocking for front with top edge ¾" from last row of stitching and design centered. From purple/blue fabric, cut one stocking for back. From fleece, cut one stocking. From purple fabric, cut two stockings for lining front and back, one 2" x 5" piece for hanger, and 1½"-wide bias strips, piecing as needed to equal 60".

2. Baste fleece to wrong side of stocking front.

3. Make piping, using cotton cord and 1½"-wide bias strips.

4. With raw edges aligned, stitch the piping down the side, around the bottom, and up the other sides of the stocking front. With right sides together, stitch the stocking front to the back, sewing along the stitching line of the piping. Leave the top edge open. Trim seams; turn.

5. With right sides facing and edges aligned, stitch the lining front and back together, leaving the top edge open and an opening in the side seam above the heel. Do not turn.

6. To make hanger, fold 2" x 5" piece in half lengthwise, with right sides facing and long edges aligned. Stitch long edges. Turn. With seam at back center, fold hanger in half. Press. With raw edges matching, pin the loop adjacent to the top right side seam of the stocking.

7. Slide the lining over the stocking, right sides together. Stitch around the top edge of the stocking, securing the hanger. Turn the stocking right side out through the side opening in the lining. Slipstitch the opening closed. Slide the lining inside the socking.

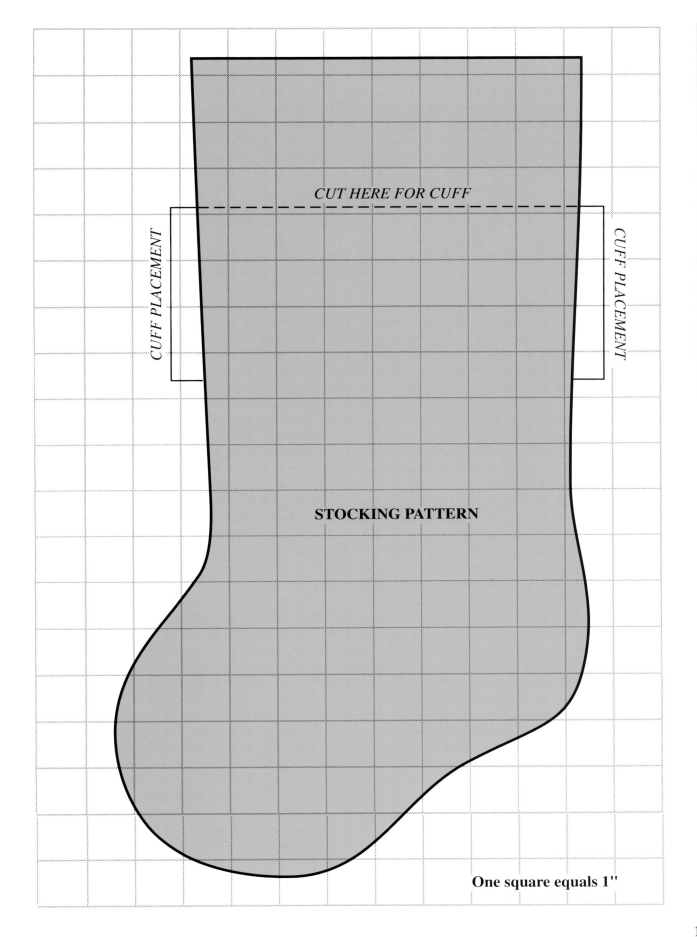

CUT HERE FOR CUFF

CUFF PLACEMENT

CUFF PLACEMENT

STOCKING PATTERN

One square equals 1"

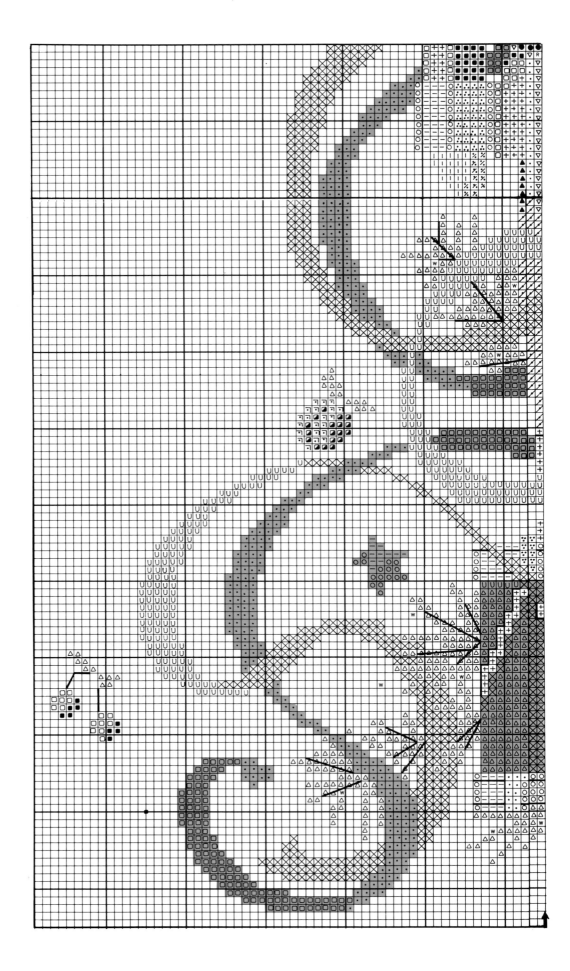

DMC   **Anchor (used for sample)**

Step 1: Cross-stitch (2 strands)

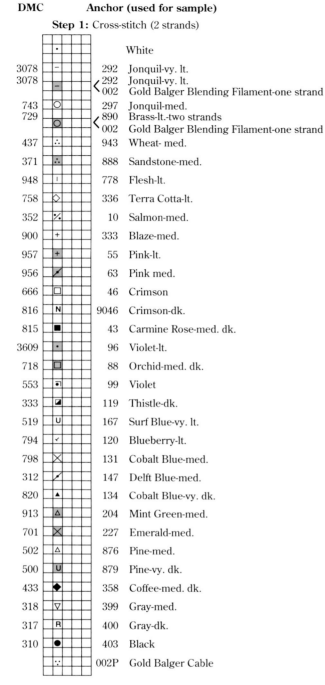

	·	White
3078	–	292 Jonquil-vy. lt.
3078	▬	292 Jonquil-vy. lt. / 002 Gold Balger Blending Filament-one strand
743	○	297 Jonquil-med.
729	◉	890 Brass-lt.-two strands / 002 Gold Balger Blending Filament-one strand
437	∴	943 Wheat- med.
371	∴	888 Sandstone-med.
948	ı	778 Flesh-lt.
758	◇	336 Terra Cotta-lt.
352	%.	10 Salmon-med.
900	+	333 Blaze-med.
957	+	55 Pink-lt.
956	◢	63 Pink med.
666	□	46 Crimson
816	N	9046 Crimson-dk.
815	■	43 Carmine Rose-med. dk.
3609	·	96 Violet-lt.
718	▢	88 Orchid-med. dk.
553	◪	99 Violet
333	◪	119 Thistle-dk.
519	U	167 Surf Blue-vy. lt.
794	˅	120 Blueberry-lt.
798	✕	131 Cobalt Blue-med.
312	╱	147 Delft Blue-med.
820	▲	134 Cobalt Blue-vy. dk.
913	△	204 Mint Green-med.
701	✕	227 Emerald-med.
502	△	876 Pine-med.
500	U	879 Pine-vy. dk.
433	◆	358 Coffee-med. dk.
318	▽	399 Gray-med.
317	R	400 Gray-dk.
310	●	403 Black
	∴	002P Gold Balger Cable

Step 2: Backstitch (1 strand)

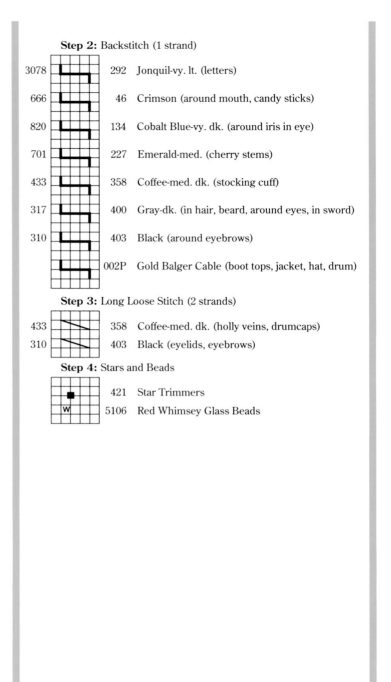

3078	292 Jonquil-vy. lt. (letters)
666	46 Crimson (around mouth, candy sticks)
820	134 Cobalt Blue-vy. dk. (around iris in eye)
701	227 Emerald-med. (cherry stems)
433	358 Coffee-med. dk. (stocking cuff)
317	400 Gray-dk. (in hair, beard, around eyes, in sword)
310	403 Black (around eyebrows)
	002P Gold Balger Cable (boot tops, jacket, hat, drum)

Step 3: Long Loose Stitch (2 strands)

| 433 | 358 Coffee-med. dk. (holly veins, drumcaps) |
| 310 | 403 Black (eyelids, eyebrows) |

Step 4: Stars and Beads

| ■ | 421 Star Trimmers |
| W | 5106 Red Whimsey Glass Beads |

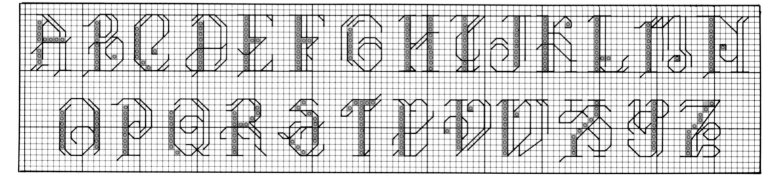

ELEGANT SCROLL CUFF STOCKING

Stitched on delft blue Aida 14 over one thread, the finished design size is 7" x 3⅛". The fabric was cut 13" x 10".

FABRICS	**DESIGN SIZES**
Aida 11	8⅞" x 4"
Aida 18	5⅛" x 2½"
Hardanger 22	4½" x 2"

MATERIALS
Completed design on blue Aida 14
½ yard of purple/blue print fabric
½ yard of purple fabric
⅜ yard of fleece
1½ yards of ³⁄₁₆" cotton cord
Blue sewing thread
Tracing paper

DIRECTIONS
All seams are ½".

1. Enlarge the pattern on the grid on page 103 to make a full-size pattern. Cut out. From print fabric, cut two stockings for front and back. From purple fabric, cut two stockings for lining front and back, cut one 16" x 4⅝" piece for cuff lining, cut one 2" x 5" piece for hanger, and cut 1½"-wide bias strips, piecing as needed, to equal 60". From fleece, cut one stocking front. With design piece centered, trim to 16" x 4⅝".

2. With right sides facing, sew short ends of design piece together forming a loop. Repeat on cuff lining.

3. With right sides facing, sew design piece and cuff lining together along bottom edge. Trim seams and turn right-side out. Press and set aside.

4. Baste fleece to wrong side of stocking front.

5. Make piping, using cotton cord and 1½"-wide bias strips.

6. With raw edges aligned, stitch the piping down the side, around the bottom, and up the other side of the stocking front. With right sides together, stitch the stocking front to the back, sewing along the stitching line of the piping. Leave the top edge open. Trim seams; turn.

7. Slip design fabric cuff over stocking, aligning top raw edges; baste.

8. With right sides facing and edges aligned, stitch the lining front and back together, leaving the top edge open and an opening in the side seam above the heel. Do not turn.

9. To make hanger, fold 2" x 5" piece in half lengthwise, with right sides facing and long edges aligned. Stitch long edges. Turn. With seam at back center, fold hanger in half. Press. With raw edges matching, pin the loop adjacent to the top right side seam of the stocking.

10. Slide the lining over the stocking, right sides together. Stitch around the top edge of the stocking, securing the hanger. Turn the stocking right side out through the side opening in the lining. Slipstitch the opening closed. Slide the lining inside the stocking.

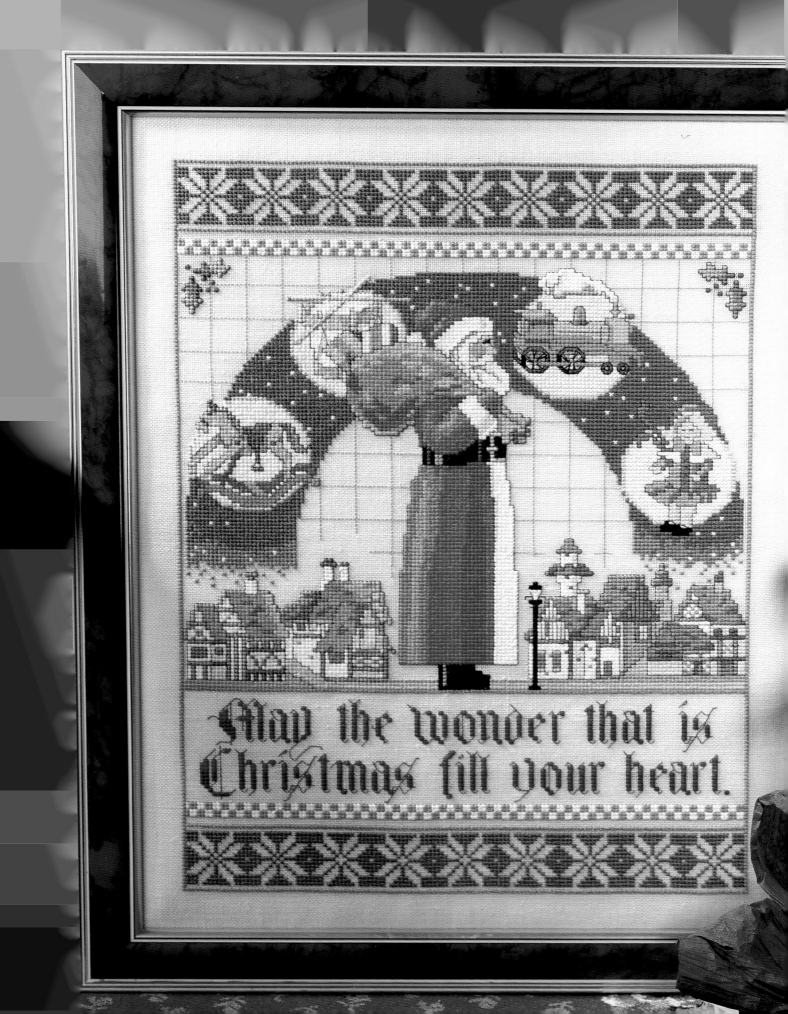

At Christmas, a child still lives in us all.
Believe in the Magic of Christmas.

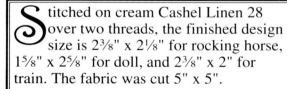
Stitched on cream Cashel Linen 28 over two threads, the finished design size is 2⅜" x 2⅛" for rocking horse, 1⅝" x 2⅝" for doll, and 2⅜" x 2" for train. The fabric was cut 5" x 5".

ROCKING HORSE

FABRICS	DESIGN SIZES
Aida 11	3" x 2⅝"
Aida 14	2⅜" x 2⅛"
Aida 18	1⅞" x 1⅝"
Hardanger 22	1½" x 1⅜"

DOLL

FABRICS	DESIGN SIZES
Aida 11	2" x 3⅜"
Aida 14	1⅝" x 2⅝"
Aida 18	1¼" x 2"
Hardanger 22	1" x 1⅝"

TRAIN

FABRICS	DESIGN SIZES
Aida 11	3" x 2½"
Aida 14	2⅜" x 2"
Aida 18	1⅞" x 1½"
Hardanger 22	1½" x 1¼"

MATERIALS *(for one ornament)*
Completed design on Cashel linen 28
¼ yard of green fabric; matching thread
3" x 4" piece of heavyweight cardboard
3" x 4" piece of lightweight cardboard
3" x 4" piece of fleece
15" of ³⁄₁₆"-diameter cotton cord
½ yard of threaded green faceted beads
Glue
Tracing paper

DIRECTIONS

1. Trace and cut out ornament pattern on page 123. From heavyweight cardboard, cut one ornament. From lightweight cardboard, cut one ornament. From fleece, cut one ornament. From green fabric, cut one ornament, adding 1" to all edges. Also from green fabric, cut 1½"-wide bias strips, piecing as needed to equal 20". With design piece centered, cut one ornament, adding 1" to all edges.

2. Lightly glue fleece to heavyweight cardboard.

3. Center fleece/cardboard over wrong side of design. Pulling snugly, wrap and glue edges to cardboard back.

4. Center lightweight cardboard over wrong side of green fabric. Pulling snugly, wrap and glue edges to cardboard back.

5. Make piping, using cotton cord and green bias strips.

6. Glue piping around back edge of design/cardboard, overlapping ends at center bottom.

7. Cut a 11½"-length of threaded beads and glue ends to prevent raveling; couch beads around design/cardboard piece along the seam of the piping and design/cardboard, overlapping ends at center bottom.

8. Cut a 5" length of bead thread. Fold length in half to form a loop for hanger and glue raw ends to back of design/cardboard at center top edge.

9. Glue wrong sides of design/cardboard and fabric/cardboard together. Weight with brick or book until glue is dry.

WINTER WONDERLAND

titched on sandstone Linen 28 over two threads, the finished design size is 10⅜" x 14¼". The fabric was cut 17" x 21".

FABRICS

Aida 11	13⅛" x 18⅛"
Aida 14	10⅜" x 14¼"
Aida 18	8⅛" x 11⅛"
Hardanger 22	6⅝" x 9⅛"

DESIGN SIZES

Anchor		DMC (used for sample)	

Step 1: Cross-stitch (2 strands)

Anchor		DMC	
1	· ⁄		White
301	⅛	744	Yellow-pale
303	▫ ⁄	742	Tangerine-lt.
316	U ⁄	740	Tangerine
891	△	676	Old Gold-lt.
890	∴	729	Old Gold-med.
881	⌐ ⁄	945	Peach Beige
74	G	3354	Dusty Rose-vy. lt.
28	▬	3706	Melon-med.
35	▲	3705	Melon-dk.
13	◉	349	Coral-dk.
59	✕	326	Rose-vy. dk.
44	⁙	814	Garnet-dk.
95	◇	554	Violet-lt.
99	◆	552	Violet-dk.
158	+ ⁄	3756	Baby Blue-ultra vy. lt.
433	▼ ⁄	996	Electric Blue-med.
121	ı	793	Cornflower Blue-med.
940	○	792	Cornflower Blue-dk.
186	▽ ⁄	959	Seagreen-med.
187	B ⁄B	958	Seagreen-dk.
214	M	368	Pistachio Green-lt.
216	▲	367	Pistachio Green-dk.
216	▲	367	Pistachio Green-dk.
256	·	906	Parrot Green-med.
347	▫	402	Mahogany-vy. lt.
338	✕	3776	Mahogany-lt.
355	■	975	Golden Brown-dk.
392	⁄	642	Beige Gray-dk.
393	∴	3790	Beige Gray-ultra vy. dk.
397	- ⁄	762	Pearl Gray-vy. lt.
399	S	318	Steel Gray-lt.
401	T	413	Pewter Gray-dk.
403	● ⁄	310	Black

Step 2: Backstitch (1 strand)

Anchor		DMC	
44		814	Garnet-dk. (berries, saying, rockers on horse, red around Santa, doll's mouth)
246		319	Pistachio Green-vy. dk. (holly, green on Santa, green on doll, green on horse)
338		3776	Mahogany-lt. (checkerboard, background squares, Santa's face)
355		975	Golden Brown-dk. (yellow on drum, train, doll's face, hair, hands, legs, Santa's belt buckle)
905		3031	Mocha Brown-vy. dk. (rocking horse, Santa's sack, brown on houses)
403		310	Black (Santa's belt, eye, boot, lampost, doll's eyes, shoes, wheels on train)
401		413	Pewter Gray-dk. (all else)

Step 3: French Knot (1 strand)

Anchor		DMC	
401	●	413	Pewter Gray-dk.

Stitch Count: 145" x 200"

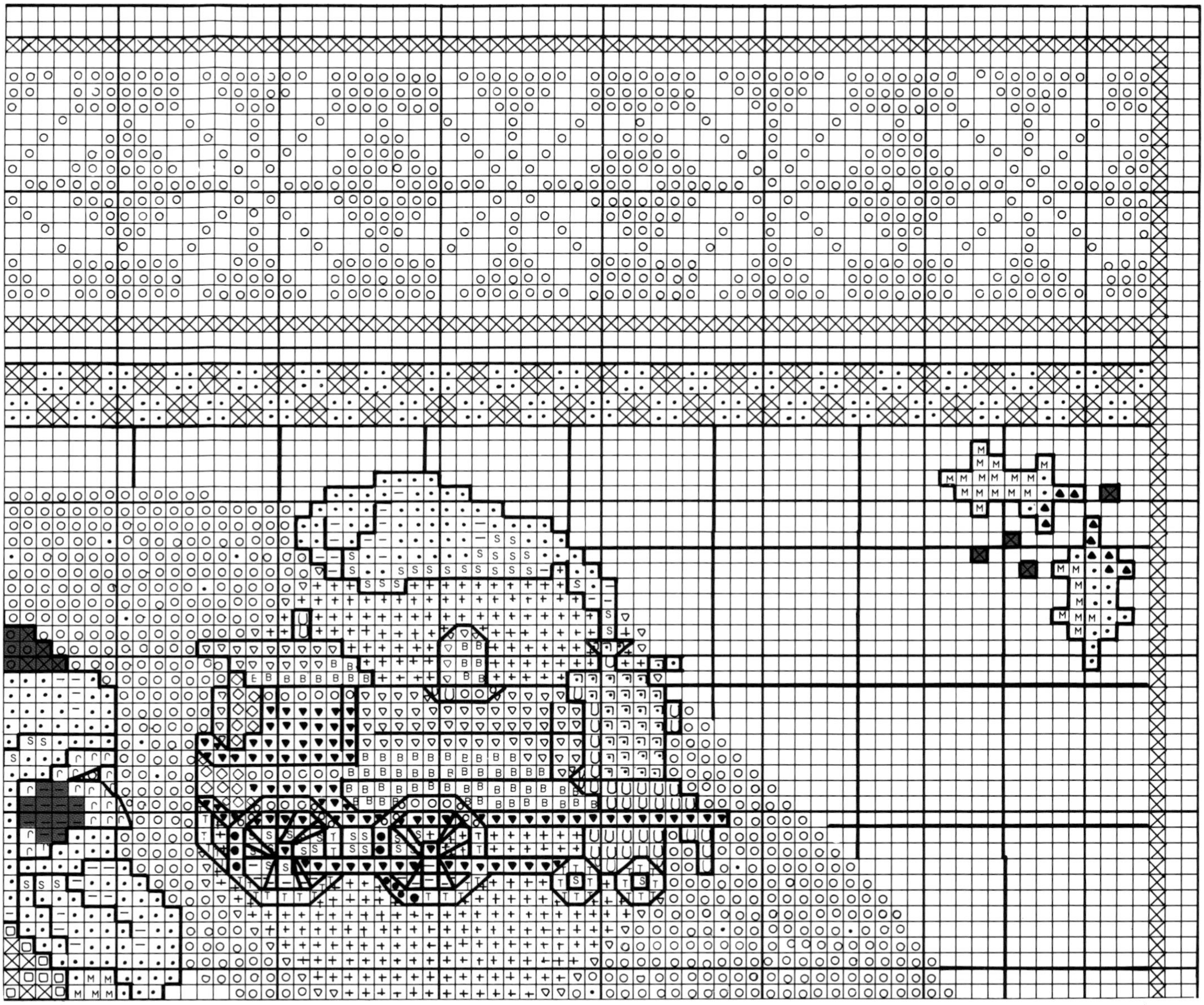

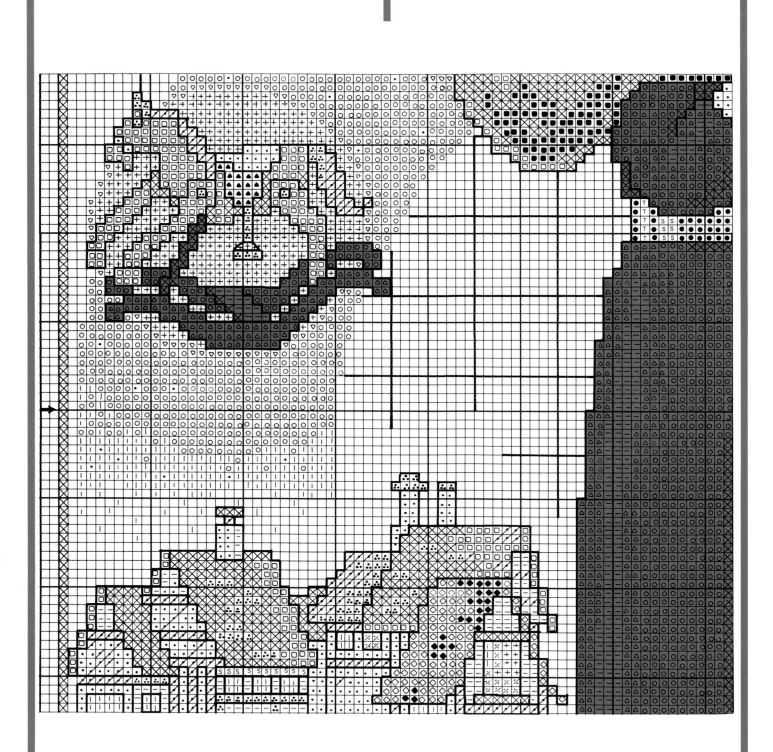

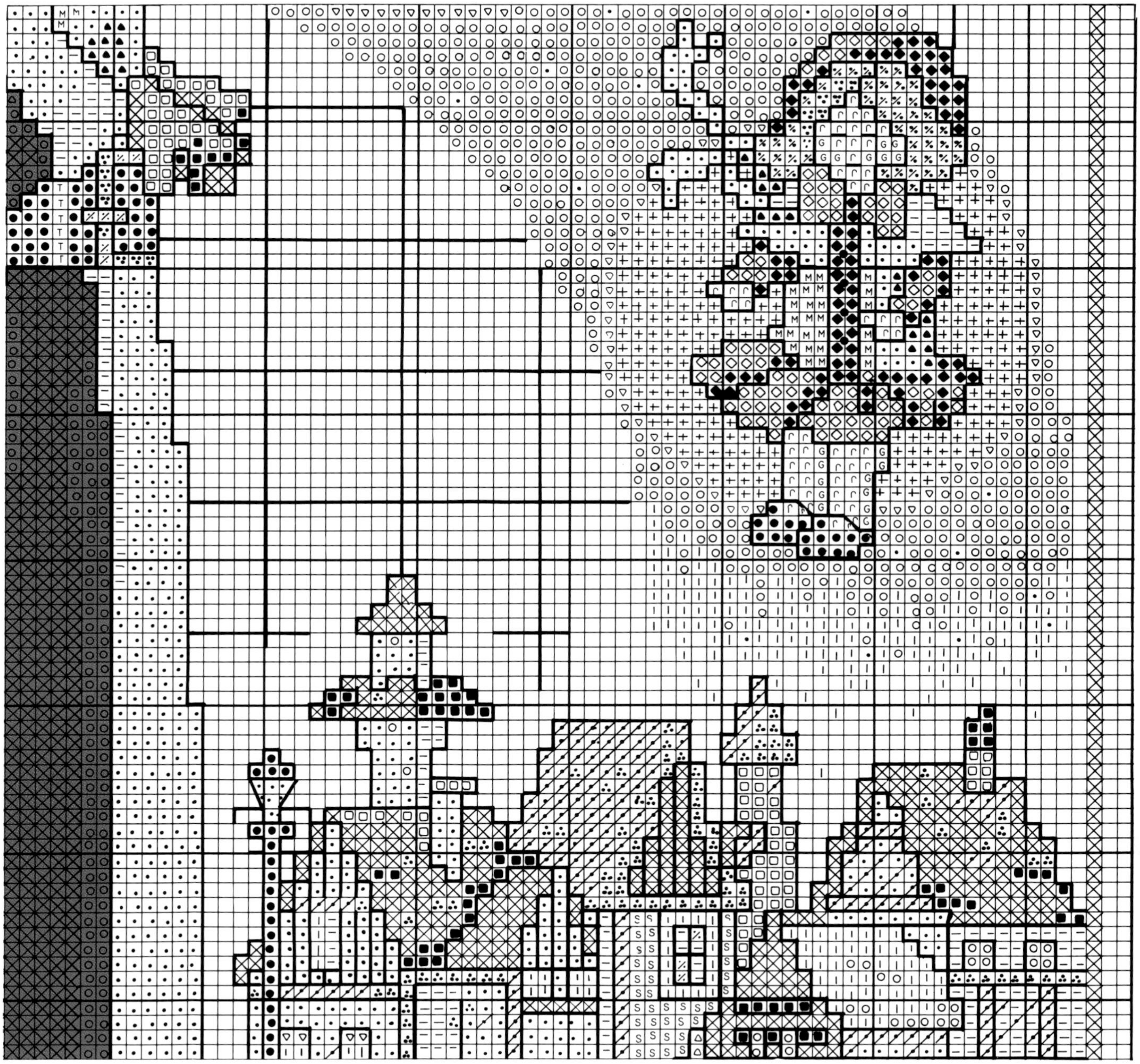

WINTER WONDERLAND TABLE LINENS

Stitched on white Aida 14 over one thread, the finished design size is 1⅜" x 1⅜" for napkin, and 1⅜" x 1⅜" for breadcloth. The fabric was cut 15" x 15" for napkin, and 18" x 18" for breadcloth. For napkin or breadcloth, begin stitching in corner ½" from edges. Stitch one snowflake motif and a single row of red cross-stitches one square from design on all sides. Repeat in each corner for breadcloth.

Stitched on white Aida 14 over one thread, the finished design size is 10½" x 1⅜" for placemat. The fabric was cut 18" x 13" for placemat. Beginning at left side of placemat ¾" from edge and centered vertically, stitch one vertical row of snowflakes and a single row of red cross-stitches one square from design on all sides.

NAPKIN

FABRICS	DESIGN SIZES
Aida 11	1¾" x 1¾"
Aida 18	1" x 1"
Hardanger 22	⅞" x ⅞"

BREADCLOTH

FABRICS	DESIGN SIZES
Aida 11	1¾" x 1¾"
Aida 18	1" x 1"
Hardanger 22	⅞" x ⅞"

PLACEMAT

FABRICS	DESIGN SIZES
Aida 11	13⅜" x 1¾"
Aida 18	8⅛" x 1"
Hardanger 22	6⅝" x ⅞"

Stitched on antique white Edinborough Linen 36 over two threads, the finished design size is 1½" x ⅞" for one motif. The fabric was cut 11" x 9".

FABRICS	DESIGN SIZES
Aida 11	2½" x 1⅜"
Aida 14	1⅞" x 1⅛"
Aida 18	1½" x ⅞"
Hardanger 22	1¼" x ⅝"

Materials

12" x 9" piece of antique white Edinborough Linen 36 for design
10" x 6" piece of antique white Edinborough Linen 36 for bib, straps, and waistband
8" square of white fabric; matching thread
1 yard of ½"-wide white flat Cluny-type lace
One small snap set

Directions

All seams are ¼".

1. From unstitched linen, cut one 1¾" x 2" piece for bib, two 7½" x 1" pieces for waistband, and four ¾" x 5" pieces for straps. From white fabric, cut one 8" x 5" piece for skirt lining and one 1¾" x 1⅝" piece for bib lining.

2. Center and baste an 8" x 5" rectangle on design piece. Stitch holly design so that bottom of design is ¾" above bottom 8" edge and centered horizontally. Trim fabric along basting line.

3. Cut one 12" length of lace and gather to 7½". Baste lace to lower edge of design fabric, allowing ½" to extend beyond bottom edge. (Lace should not extend into side edges.)

4. With right sides facing, sew design and lining pieces together, leaving top edge open. Trim corners; turn right-side out, and press. Zigzag raw edges together.

5. For bib, pin-tuck three ⅛"-deep horizontal rows, beginning ½" from 1¾" top edge of bib and spaced ⅛" apart. With right sides facing, sew bib and lining pieces together across top edge. Turn and press.

6. Cut two 8" lengths of lace and gather each to 5"; turn raw ends to back and tack. Aligning raw edges, sandwich one gathered lace length between two strap strips with right sides facing and with lace ¼" from both ends of strap; see diagram. Sew long edge, catching lace in seam. Turn and press. Repeat for other strap.

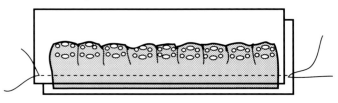

DIAGRAM

7. Sandwich one side of bib between strap strips, aligning all bottom edges. Fold raw edges of strap ¼" to the inside. Topstitch long edge and ends closed. Repeat with other side of bib and remaining strap.

8. Mark centers of lower edge of bib and both waistband strips on long edge. Sandwich bib between strips with right sides together and matching center marks. Sew one long edge and ends of waistband. Clip corners. Turn waistband; press.

9. Sew gathering thread ⅛" from top of design. Mark center and gather to 4". Sandwich design between waistband strips with right sides facing and matching centers. Fold raw edge of waistband under ¼". Slipstitch long edge.

10. Tack ends of shoulder straps to back of waistband. Sew snap set to ends of waistband.

Stitch Count: 27" x 15"

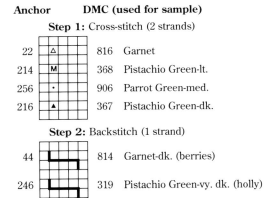

Anchor   **DMC (used for sample)**

Step 1: Cross-stitch (2 strands)

Anchor	Symbol	DMC	Color
22	△	816	Garnet
214	M	368	Pistachio Green-lt.
256	·	906	Parrot Green-med.
216	▲	367	Pistachio Green-dk.

Step 2: Backstitch (1 strand)

Anchor		DMC	Color
44		814	Garnet-dk. (berries)
246		319	Pistachio Green-vy. dk. (holly)

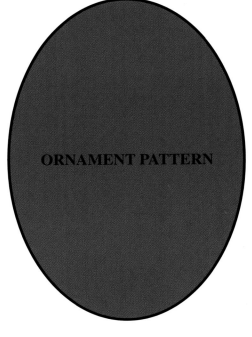

Pattern for Winter Wonderland Ornaments on page 112.

GENERAL INSTRUCTIONS

CROSS-STITCH

Fabrics: Counted cross-stitch is usually worked on even-weave fabric. These fabrics are manufactured specifically for counted-thread embroidery and are woven with the same number of vertical as horizontal threads per inch. Because the number of threads in the fabric is equal in each direction, each stitch will be the same size. It is the number of threads per inch in even-weave fabrics that determines the size of a finished design.

Waste Canvas: Waste canvas is a coarse, fabric-like substance used as a guide for cross-stitching on fabrics other than even-weaves. Cut the waste canvas 1" larger on all sides than the finished design size. Baste it to the fabric to be stitched. Complete the stitching. Then, dampen the stitched area with cold water. Pull the waste canvas threads out one at a time with tweezers. It is easier to pull all the threads running in one direction first, then pull out the opposite threads. Allow the stitching to dry. Place face down on a towel and iron.

Preparing Fabric: Cut even-weave fabric at least 3" larger on all sides than the design size, or cut it the size specified in the instructions. If the item is to be finished into a pillow, for example, the fabric should be cut as directed. A 3" margin is the minimum amount of space that allows for comfortably working the edges of the design. To prevent fraying, whipstitch or machine-zigzag raw fabric edges.

Needles: Needles should slip easily through the holes in the fabric but not pierce the fabric. Use a blunt tapestry needle, size 24 or 26. Never leave the needle in the design area of your work. It can leave rust or a permanent impression on the fabric.

Floss: All numbers and color names are cross-referenced between Anchor and DMC brands of floss. Run the floss over a damp sponge to straighten. Separate all six strands and use the number of strands called for in the code.

Centering the Design: Fold the fabric in half horizontally, then vertically. Place a pin in the fold point to mark the center. Locate the center of the design on the graph by following the vertical and horizontal arrows in the left and bottom margins. Begin stitching all designs at the center point of the graph and the fabric unless the instructions indicate otherwise.

Graphs: Each symbol represents a different color. Make one stitch for each symbol, referring to the code to verify which stitch to use. Use the small arrows in the margins to find the center of the graph. When a graph is continued, the bottom two rows of the graph on the previous page are repeated, separated by a small space, indicating where to connect them. The stitch count is printed with each graph, listing first the width, then the length, of the design.

Codes:
The code indicates the brand of thread used to stitch the model, as well as the cross-reference for using another brand. The steps in the code identify the stitch to be used and the number of floss strands for that stitch. The symbols match the graph, and give the color number and name for the thread. A symbol under a diagonal line indicates a half-cross-stitch. Blended threads are represented on the code and graph with a single symbol, but both color names are listed.

Securing the Floss:
Insert your needle up from the underside of the fabric at your starting point. Hold 1" of thread behind the fabric and stitch over it, securing with the first few stitches. To finish thread, run under four or more stitches on the back of the design. Never knot floss unless working on clothing. Another method of securing floss is the waste knot. Knot your floss and insert your needle from the right side of the fabric about 1" from design area. Work several stitches over the thread to secure. Cut off the knot later.

Stitching:
For a smooth cross-stitch, use the "push-and-pull" method. Push the needle straight down and completely through fabric before pulling. Do not pull the thread tightly. Consistent tension throughout ensures even stitches. Make one stitch for every symbol on the chart. To stitch in rows, work from left to right and then back. Half-crosses are used to make a rounded shape. Make the longer stitch in the direction of the slanted line.

Carrying Floss:
To carry floss, weave floss under the previously worked stitches on the back. Do not carry thread across any fabric that is not or will not be stitched. Loose threads, especially dark ones, will show through the fabric.

Twisted Floss:
If floss is twisted, drop the needle and allow the floss to unwind itself. Floss will cover best when lying flat. Use thread no longer than 18" because it will tend to twist and knot.

Cleaning Completed Work:
When stitching is complete, soak it in cold water with a mild soap for five to ten minutes. Rinse well and roll in a towel to remove excess water. Do not wring. Place work face down on a dry towel and iron on a warm setting until dry.

Cross-stitch:
Make one cross for each symbol on the chart. Bring needle and thread up at A, down at B, up at C, and down again at D. For rows, stitch from left to right, then back. All stitches should lie in the same direction.

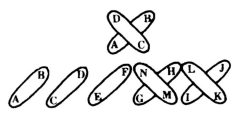

Half-cross-stitch:
The stitch actually fits three-fourths of the area. Make the longer stitch in the direction of the slanted line on the graph. Bring needle and thread up at A, down at B, up at C, and down at D.

Backstitch:
Complete all cross-stitching before working backstitches or other accent stitches. Working from left to right with one strand of floss (unless designated otherwise on code), bring needle and thread up at A, down at B, and up again at C. Go back down at A and continue in this manner.

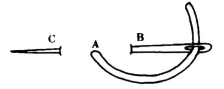

125

French Knot:
Bring needle up at A, using one strand of embroidery floss. Wrap floss around needle two times (unless indicated otherwise in instructions). Insert needle beside A, pulling floss until it fits snugly around needle. Pull needle through to back.

Sewing Hints

Patterns:
Use tracing paper to trace patterns. Be sure to transfer all information. All patterns include seam allowances. The seam allowance is ¼" unless otherwise specified.

Marking on Fabric:
Always use a dressmaker's pen or chalk to mark on fabric. It will wash out when you clean your finished piece.

Slipstitch:
Insert needle at A, taking a small stitch, and slide it through the folded edge of the fabric about ⅛" to ¼", bringing it out at B.

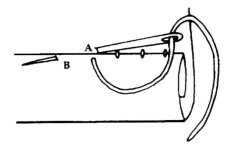

Enlarging a Pattern:
On a sheet of paper large enough to hold the finished pattern, mark grid lines 1" apart to fill the paper. Begin marking dots on 1" grid lines where the reduced pattern intersects the corresponding grid line. Connect the dots. Fabric stores sell pattern-making products which can save a great deal of time.

Bias Strips:
Bias strips are used for ruffles, binding or corded piping. To cut bias, fold the fabric at a 45-degree angle to the grain of the fabric and crease. Cut on the crease. Cut additional strips the width indicated in the instructions and parallel to the first cutting line. The ends of the bias strips should be on the grain of the fabric. Place the right sides of the ends together and stitch with a ¼" seam. Continue to piece the strips until they are the length that is indicated in the instructions.

Corded Piping:
Center cording on the wrong side of the bias strip and fold the fabric over it, aligning raw edges. Using a zipper foot, stitch through both layers of fabric close to the cording. Trim the seam allowance to ¼".

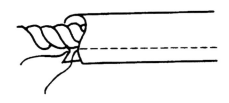

Mitering a Corner:
Sew border strips up to but not through the seam allowance; backstitch. Repeat on all four edges, making stitching lines meet exactly at the corners. Fold two adjacent border pieces together. Mark, then stitch at a 45-degree angle. Trim seam allowance to ¼".

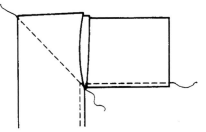

METRIC EQUIVALENCY CHART

MM-Millimetres   CM-Centimetres

INCHES TO MILLIMETRES AND CENTIMETRES

INCHES	MM	CM	INCHES	CM	INCHES	CM
⅛	3	0.3	9	22.9	30	76.2
¼	6	0.6	10	25.4	31	78.7
½	13	1.3	12	30.5	33	83.8
⅝	16	1.6	13	33.0	34	86.4
¾	19	1.9	14	35.6	35	88.9
⅞	22	2.2	15	38.1	36	91.4
1	25	2.5	16	40.6	37	94.0
1¼	32	3.2	17	43.2	38	96.5
1½	38	3.8	18	45.7	39	99.1
1¾	44	4.4	19	48.3	40	101.6
2	51	5.1	20	50.8	41	104.1
2½	64	6.4	21	53.3	42	106.7
3	76	7.6	22	55.9	43	109.2
3½	89	8.9	23	58.4	44	111.8
4	102	10.2	24	61.0	45	114.3
4½	114	11.4	25	63.5	46	116.8
5	127	12.7	26	66.0	47	119.4
6	152	15.2	27	68.6	48	121.9
7	178	17.8	28	71.1	49	124.5
8	203	20.3	29	73.7	50	127.0

YARDS TO METRES

YARDS	METRES	YARDS	METRES	YARDS	METRES	YARDS	METRES	YARDS	METRES
⅛	0.11	2⅛	1.94	4⅛	3.77	6⅛	5.60	8⅛	7.43
¼	0.23	2¼	2.06	4¼	3.89	6¼	5.72	8¼	7.54
⅜	0.34	2⅜	2.17	4⅜	4.00	6⅜	5.83	8⅜	7.66
½	0.46	2½	2.29	4½	4.11	6½	5.94	8½	7.77
⅝	0.57	2⅝	2.40	4⅝	4.23	6⅝	6.06	8⅝	7.89
¾	0.69	2¾	2.51	4¾	4.34	6¾	6.17	8¾	8.00
⅞	0.80	2⅞	2.63	4⅞	4.46	6⅞	6.29	8⅞	8.12
1	0.91	3	2.74	5	4.57	7	6.40	9	8.23
1⅛	1.03	3⅛	2.86	5⅛	4.69	7⅛	6.52	9⅛	8.34
1¼	1.14	3¼	2.97	5¼	4.80	7¼	6.63	9¼	8.46
1⅜	1.26	3⅜	3.09	5⅜	4.91	7⅜	6.74	9⅜	8.57
1½	1.37	3½	3.20	5½	5.03	7½	6.86	9½	8.69
1⅝	1.49	3⅝	3.31	5⅝	5.14	7⅝	6.97	9⅝	8.80
1¾	1.60	3¾	3.43	5¾	5.26	7¾	7.09	9¾	8.92
1⅞	1.71	3⅞	3.54	5⅞	5.37	7⅞	7.20	9⅞	9.03
2	1.83	4	3.66	6	5.49	8	7.32	10	9.14

INDEX